More Praise for *Quality Management in Learning and Development*

T0309060

"If your approach to quality assurance is a checklist at the end of your course, it's time to pick up a copy of this book and rethink your strategy. Hadiya will guide you through a tactical approach to ensuring quality in your training with a thoughtful process and practical examples."

—**Sarah Mercier,** CEO, Build Capable

"Hadiya Nuriddin has written a must-read primer that proves why an L&D team cannot survive (let alone succeed) without an informed process in place to identify and address mistakes. Through industry insights (and an engaging case study providing a solid example throughout), this book walks you through defining, planning for, assuring, and controlling quality in your learning programs—a surefire way to increase the value of the L&D function in the eyes of business leaders, stakeholders, and learners."

—**Karin Rex,** Chief Geek, Geeky Girl

"This is a must read for all organizations that care about delivering quality content to their learners. Hadiya, always a storyteller, makes an otherwise mundane task like quality management interesting and insightful."

—**Daniel Keckan,** CEO, Cinécraft Productions

"*Quality Management in Learning and Development* is a comprehensive toolkit for excelling in the e-learning sphere. Hadiya has brilliantly bridged the gap between theory and practice by providing actionable steps for quality improvement!"

—**Garima Gupta,** Founder and CEO, Artha Learning

"*Quality Management in Learning and Development* profoundly addresses the central aspects of quality management with an eloquent balance of rigor, scope, and tangible cases. It will challenge you to rethink your quality management practices, inspire you to improve upon them, and provide you with a practical road map for you and your team to co-create a shared meaning, mission, and approach to integrating a quality management system into your workflows."

—**Kristin Torrence,** Head of Learning Engineering, Talespin

"This book came at the perfect time, aligning seamlessly with my team's current initiative to enhance our quality management system. The inclusion of a detailed case study not only grounds the theoretical concepts in a practical application but also provides a clear, step-by-step blueprint that illuminates the path to an optimized and effective quality management system."

—**Tabatha Dragonberry**, Senior Instructional Designer, USAA

"As an L&D professional, you understand the value of quality products, but Hadiya immediately gets you thinking about a holistic quality-first mindset. With evidence-based research, *Quality Management in Learning and Development* takes you on a journey that covers the entire spectrum from policy to procedures, strategies, and production. This book is the one you didn't know you needed."

—**Kevin Thorn**, EdD, Director of Development, Artisan Learning

"Looking to move away from endless review cycles, inconsistent learning design, and haphazard quality processes? L&D managers, senior IDs, and anyone working to improve the training their team creates will benefit from following this systematic, sustainable, and proactive approach to quality management."

—**Christy Tucker**, Learning Experience Design Consultant, Syniad Learning

"Hadiya offers an essential and accessible guide for any learning professional committed to ensuring quality in the development of learning experiences. I'm now excited to further define my team's quality management system—something I never thought I would say!"

—**Meg Bertapelle**, Senior Instructional Designer

"Hadiya's writing drew me in immediately. Her engaging real-life experiences mirrored many of the same work situations I've faced. Pairing her art of storytelling with the underlying principles behind quality management, she makes the topic approachable for anyone in L&D. Plus, as a reader, you are left with practical tips, guides, and worksheets you can immediately apply in your workplace to create your own quality management system."

—**Tracy Parish**, Instructional Designer and Consultant, Parish Creative Solutions

"Never before has there been such solid attention on quality management in L&D until now. Hadiya's perspective on this matter is what generations of learning professionals will reverently refer to as the cornerstone of their practice."

—**Tameka J. Harris,** Pro Learning Design Strategist, IDSuccess Design Studio

"It's one thing to design a great learning solution—but without a focus on quality, what you produce may fall flat. Hadiya lays out specific tactics you can apply to your learning projects from day one to ensure quality across all layers of the experience and process. This book is a must have on any L&D professional's reading list!"

—**Cammy Bean,** Senior Solutions Consultant, Kineo; Author, *The Accidental Instructional Designer*

Quality Management
in Learning and Development

HADIYA NURIDDIN

PRESS

Alexandria, VA

ATD Press is an internationally renowned source of insightful and practical information on talent development, training, and professional development.

ATD Press
1640 King Street
Alexandria, VA 22314 USA

Ordering information: Books published by ATD Press can be purchased by visiting ATD's website at td.org/books or by calling 800.628.2783 or 703.683.8100.

Library of Congress Control Number: 2023952369

ISBN-10: 1-95394-660-7
ISBN-13: 978-1-953946-60-7
e-ISBN: 978-1-95394-684-3

ATD Press Editorial Staff
Director: Sarah Halgas
Manager: Melissa Jones
Content Manager, Learning Technologies: Alexandria Clapp
Developmental Editor: Jack Harlow
Production Editor: Katy Wiley Stewts
Text Designer: Shirley E.M. Raybuck
Text Layout: Kathleen Dyson
Cover Designer: Rose Richey

Printed by BR Printers, San Jose, CA

Contents

Introduction

I was introduced to learning and development (L&D) during my first corporate job working as a technical support representative for a software company. It had no training department, so the senior product representatives provided weekly lectures on the products we supported. However, very little training was provided to support the software in which the product resided, a confusing decision given that the technical support team routinely hired people with no technical expertise. Our technical training consisted of senior team members telling us what to do, listening in on our calls while we did it, and giving us feedback on how well it was done. Most of us learned our jobs eventually, but it was a slow and frustrating process for both the technical support representative and the customer.

Once I became a senior employee, I decided we could do better for our team and customers. I created a comprehensive curriculum that included courses on Microsoft Windows 3.1 and software troubleshooting strategies. How could I suddenly create effective training with no models or guidance? I couldn't. How do I know? Well, while delivering the course on Microsoft Windows, I fell asleep. Yes, I fell asleep while I was talking. While I could have fallen asleep for various reasons, and the course may have been effective if I had remained conscious long enough to deliver it, I suspect that's when I learned that training was more than talking.

I created technical support training by copying what I had seen before and filling in the blanks with guesses. For years after formally becoming an instructional designer, I was still guessing. Even after completing degrees and certifications in learning and development, each new job seemed to require more guessing about what my manager, clients, and team members wanted. I soon accepted that learning design is treated more as an art than the science it is, so individual people are free to decide how to best support learning. This inconsistency across industries, companies, teams, and people is frustrating, and makes me question what *professionalization* means in learning and development. It also compromises quality, which depends on a consistent, specific definition that describes expectations.

It's not that quality is being ignored in learning and development. That's impossible. As I'll mention throughout this book, an L&D team can't survive without some process for identifying and addressing mistakes. The challenge is that when discussing quality for L&D, the conversation often drifts to typos, grammatical errors, and broken links, and then stays there. In my experience, teams focus quality efforts on the post-production hunt for errors and call it *quality control* or just *review*. And this work is important. I used to say that one way to find a typo in a participant guide is to print 100 copies, open one, and flip to any page. That random page you wrote and rewrote will inevitably contain an overlooked typo that jumps off the page directly into the pit of your stomach. It's happened to me more times than I'd like to admit. What follows may be a series of calculations weighing the typo's severity against the odds of people discovering it. Perhaps you consider rewriting and reprinting the document or just confessing to the class that there may be typos and asking for forgiveness in advance.

A typo, whether minor or major, is still an error that can negatively influence your learning experience's quality. All errors have consequences, but the severity depends on the impact. Broken hyperlinks or slides with buttons leading nowhere can compromise organizational outcomes if learners can't complete e-learning courses. Unexpected silent or blank screens due to temporarily hidden text, images, or audio that were not caught before publication and distribution can cause frustration and disengagement when learners encounter them in the learning experience. Courses not adhering to accessibility standards can exclude learners from the experience entirely.

And, most egregious, learning programs that do not meet their objectives and have little impact can diminish the value of the L&D function within the eyes of business leaders, stakeholders, and learners.

The Value of Quality Management

Before you begin the journey into quality management, there's a question you need to answer for yourself and, ultimately, your organization: What's at stake? As you build your quality management system, regardless of complexity level, some will ask whether this is overkill. Like someone said to me once, "If there's a typo, fix it." The implication is that there's no need to go through the process of building a system just to insert a comma where needed. Is this really that important? In some cases, the naysayers may be correct.

You do not want to build a solution in search of a problem. The point of this exercise is not to have a quality management system. It's to address the current practices that reduce quality, slow production, and increase costs. Quality management is only one comprehensive way of taking control of your production process. So, the question of value is answered by understanding how much risk the L&D function takes on by maintaining the status quo. Again, for some teams, the risks are minimal, or the systems you're using now are enough. For other teams, they already know that the weight of the risk is enormous. However, the teams with the most significant challenge are the ones that have no idea what the issues are and what their presence is costing them.

While cosmetic and technical errors can usually be fixed when they're identified, ineffectiveness is often more challenging to address without a system. About five years into my instructional design career, I designed and developed a payroll course that was part of an organization-wide human resources software rollout. The consultants gave me the instructions and access to a dummy version of the software. With very little oversight, I did what I thought was best. I wrote down the instructions, and then told them to the participants during the training while they followed along. We all relied on me knowing what I was doing, simply because of my title and department. This was payroll training! The gravity of the situation didn't hit me until years later. I rarely get news that my training wasn't effective, but this was an exception. I found out that they believed the manual I created was unusable and subsequently created their own. I shudder to imagine what led to the moment when they decided enough was enough.

Developing the training and accompanying materials for that payroll module had far-reaching consequences. Some could argue, "Well, Hadiya. Perhaps you were just bad at your job, too new to understand what you were doing, or poorly managed." While those are all plausible reasons for the breakdown, they aren't specific enough to do anything about them. We should know exactly what happened, what was expected of everyone involved, and where the breakdown occurred. Without processes in place, it's difficult to pinpoint problems and address them. Quality management is one of those systems that can help reveal what lies beneath the work we do every day.

Quality issues are typically symptoms of larger problems triggered and proliferated by how teams are staffed, managed, and supported. For example, the quality issues plaguing some of our learning experiences are caused by a lack of evidence-based, documented, and consistently applied standards. During the decades I've worked in learning and development, the solution to addressing quality was constantly reviewing our work. Quality management consisted solely of fixing the errors reviewers, approvers, subject matter experts (SMEs), and ultimately, learners found. Some may consider this seemingly never-ending cycle of checking-and-redoing effective. After all, you will inevitably create a course with fewer errors than you would have without this process. However, conducting quality management this way is also inefficient, expensive, and often demoralizing.

It's time for all L&D teams to formally embrace quality management as an essential part of the learning experience design function. The American Society for Quality (ASQ) defines *quality management* as "all activities of the overall management function that determine the quality policy, objectives, and responsibilities, and the implementation of these by means such as quality planning, quality control, quality assurance, and quality improvement within the quality system" (Duffy and Furterer 2020). This requires shifting to a quality-first mentality and building, implementing, and supporting all the processes and procedures necessary to support that vision.

While the actual value of quality management is a data-driven decision, there is something even more significant to consider. When it's late in the day and an e-learning developer is completing the final version of a module on customer service, it's easy to see that as the end when you reflect on the module's journey. But it's only the beginning—the module should shift or support a specific set of behaviors at the site. And there are consequences depending on whether or not the shift happens. When retail associates engage with that module, they won't know if the SME commandeered the design process or the timeline was cut by a week. They just know that the module came from the training department. That's all leadership sees too. So, if the shift in behavior does not occur, the fault, right or wrong, falls on us.

The customer knows even less. All they see is a cashier, Todd, at a register; whether he follows the protocol he learned from the training module will heavily influence the customer experience. And, of course, it determines whether that customer returns and how they will talk about their time with Todd. That customer's experience will influence the retail organization's bottom line.

A process with that significant of an impact deserves its own support. It deserves its own quality standard, guidelines, and processes that can be reviewed, modified, and updated. Many times, I had to build training for other departments for processes that were not documented. I once worked with a global advertising company to implement new software that would affect one specific team's work. Nothing was documented, and everyone on the team was doing the job differently. Consequently, the company wanted to use the learning design process to figure out the current processes for the job and then teach people how to do the job using the new software. I was shocked that, in such a large company, no one seemed to know what an entire team was doing, that there was no consistency, and that nothing was documented. Yet, many of us in L&D work under the same circumstances while simultaneously "process shaming" other organizations for doing the same.

Who Is This Book For?

I've had the opportunity to experience quality management from different perspectives. As an instructional designer and developer, it was my job to ensure my materials were perfect. As a manager, I tried to provide the support my team needed to ensure the materials they created were perfect. As an instructional design instructor, I reinforced the idea that the responsibility fell on the instructional designer's shoulders to ensure everything they created was perfect. And as a freelance consultant, it fell on me to ensure that all my materials were, again, perfect.

I was never told, and I never asked or considered what, beyond accuracy, *perfect* meant. I also never questioned whose responsibility it was to reach this mythical peak. Consequently, there was no clear plan to get there. The truth is that in all the different roles I played, it was my responsibility, but also everyone else's. Quality is not just about what you produce—it's about who you are as part of a learning organization because the quest for quality should influence every decision. Your team's commitment to quality reflects your commitment to your learners. Your commitment to your learners reflects your commitment to the organization's success. And your commitment to the organization is why your team exists.

Ultimately, this book is for everyone in learning and development because we all play a role in shaping the learner experience. But it's primarily for the person tasked with building or reinforcing the bridge to quality management. This person could be at any level and hold any internal or external L&D role. It's for the senior instructional designer looking for ways to reduce the amount of revisions that need to be done. It's for the new instructional designer who wants to understand what standard they will, or should be, held to. It's for the learning management system administrator who wants to reduce the frequency of uploading revised courses. It's for freelancers who want to provide their clients with a better experience when reviewing materials. Finally, it's for the L&D manager who wants to demonstrate their team's commitment to the organization's health.

However, while anyone at any level can lead and champion the creation of a quality management system, this book will stress the importance of senior management input and support. According to ASQ, "An essential first step in getting started on process improvement is when senior management makes it a strategic organizational goal. The importance of process improvement must be communicated from the top. Leaders need to foster an organizational environment in which process improvement can thrive and people are regularly using techniques and tools related to quality improvement" (Duffy and Furterer 2020). In other words, while this effort can be built from the bottom up, it must be sustained from the top down.

Note that this book focuses on quality for learning materials developed for adult learners in the business sector, including corporations, nonprofit organizations, and associations. While this definition does not include materials created for K–12 or higher education, teams that create professional development opportunities for staff and faculty can also benefit from the methods explored here.

What's in This Book?

The goal of this book is not to simply develop and implement a quality management system, but to use its guidance to learn more about how the learning experiences your team produces support your organization and how well-supported your team is when doing so. Ideally, this journey of discovery will unearth new or improved strategies for meeting the team's collective vision of quality. Developing and implementing a quality management system is just one way to meet that challenge.

Chapter 1 provides a brief history of quality management and an overview of quality as a term, concept, and discipline. In addition, I'll explore the benefits of implementing quality management systems or formalizing the systems you already have.

Chapter 2 explores the components of a quality management system and the role of each process. It's a level- and expectation-setting exercise about process inputs and outputs, what's expected of whom, and what outcomes you, your team, and your organization can anticipate.

In chapter 3, I transition from discussing quality in the abstract to looking at it through the lens of learning and development. I'll consider what quality management looks like in L&D and how to prepare to begin the journey. I'll also introduce a case study featuring an L&D manager that I'll use to provide background for the examples that appear throughout the book.

In chapter 4, I'll explore strategies for identifying what quality means for you and your team. This exercise includes gaining a clear understanding of the current state of your work and where you ultimately want to be. Ideally, you'll develop goals or a mission statement that supports your team's philosophy about the value it adds to improving performance at your organization.

Chapter 5 focuses on planning for quality. Once you have your mission and goals, you will enter the planning phase and develop a project plan and team to move forward. Developing a quality management system is a challenging process best navigated by teams that are equally committed and understand what lies ahead.

Chapter 6 focuses on defining a standard and its role in quality management. I'll review other standards from related industries that you can use to inform your own standard. Then, I'll discuss how to develop guidelines that support the standard. I'll explore how to find existing guidelines and create and structure new ones.

Many associate quality control with a checklist designed to help reviewers identify postproduction errors. However, it's difficult to control quality after a product has been created. Quality control happens during course creation, not after—it's the policies and procedures created to support the guidelines designers and developers should follow. In chapter 7, you'll learn how to create the policies and procedures needed to support compliance.

Quality review is a more appropriate name for postdevelopment reviews. Chapter 8 will explore strategies for creating an effective and sustainable review process.

Chapter 9 is devoted to reviewing answers to frequently asked questions about developing, customizing, adapting, and maintaining a quality management system.

Finally, the appendix includes templates and tools you can use as you build and support your quality management system.

Throughout the book, you'll also find some additional notes and tips. The notes provide some extra information about the section they appear in, and the tips offer some best practices for you to implement in your team.

Ready to get started? As you'll soon learn, commitment is the first step on this journey. By reading this book, you've accepted the challenge to pave a path to an effective and sustainable quality culture within your practice and the organizations you serve. Remember, if you are building the process in the face of doubt, or if initial team enthusiasm begins to wane, the time you take to build a quality management system is an investment in your learners, your team, your organization, and ultimately, in your career as an L&D professional.

CHAPTER 1
Introduction to Quality Management

IN THIS CHAPTER:
- Quality management defined
- A brief history of quality management
- Benefits of implementing a quality management system

In L&D, we create presentations, workbooks, reference guides, digital products, and many other items. We refer to them by their function, but ultimately, they are all products that take time, effort, and skill to design and produce. Production of any item is typically improved by following a consistently applied process, which helps ensure that each one is created in a uniform way, minimizing variations and defects. The oversight that standardization provides often results in more reliable products, boosting customer confidence and streamlining troubleshooting when issues arise.

L&D products are not immune to needing strategic oversight. We make decisions similar to those in other industries. Are you building a car? No, but you may be designing and developing products that support those who do. Errors in their training and reference materials influence a worker's ability to build cars successfully, so why shouldn't our products be subject to rigorous protocols as well?

During my time working in technical support, in addition to training and technology, I learned about the concept of quality itself. It remains the most influential era of my career because I learned about consequences—how one decision you make may affect an entire network and all the people who depend on it. I was also introduced to the idea that quality doesn't just happen when you're being careful and working hard. Quality has to be systematically controlled.

In my first technical support position, I worked at a help desk for a financial software company. I had no insight into how they managed software production, but the decisions made during that process directly influenced the technical support team. The company mailed new software (on 10 floppy disks!) every month that subscribers then installed themselves. In nearly half of the 12 releases a year, customers would experience problems after installing the product ranging from the software repeatedly crashing to the subscriber's computer no longer booting into Microsoft Windows.

The company had a software quality management team. In fact, the technical support manager often loaned out my team members to the quality management team to assist in running through test scripts. It was tedious, but it made us more sympathetic to the developers' plight. In retrospect, garnering empathy from the technical support team may have been the objective, because we often complained about the subscriber's frustrations.

As a learning designer and e-learning developer, I often reflect on my days in technical support and my introduction to quality testing. I think about releasing products with good intentions—knowing you've checked every screen, button, and word—yet clients still experience the unexpected. I've even grown to appreciate my previous employer's laborious quality testing exercise because the process was at least documented and structured with instructions and expectations so clear that the process could be handed off to a newbie who had only been working with technology for a year. However, regardless of my efforts, I'm sure that some of the features I tested myself still contained errors.

Starting at the Beginning

We all knew how my previous employer's financial software was supposed to function. The software was coded according to specifications dictated by a standard for how subscribers gain value from the tool. We were testing against the standard's guidelines. Without them, we could only test against our assumptions or expectations. You may have experienced a similar situation with new gadgets or software. You fumble your way through the process based on expectations, and if something doesn't meet them, you don't know whether you're wrong or the device is not working. It's always helpful to have some idea of how something is supposed to work. A printer should print. If you double-click an icon, the corresponding software program should open. But what if there is no specific way for the object to function? How can you determine whether something met your expectations if you don't know what to expect?

Quality management begins with crafting your team's quality management mission, which is influenced by your team's goals regarding quality and the type of product or service being evaluated. Next, you develop a standard to support the mission. Guidelines then support the standard. In fact, the standard is primarily a collection of guidelines. For example, suppose one element of your team's mission is supporting employees beyond the structured learning experience. To enforce that mission, the team creates a guideline within the standard stating that every learning experience will include an easily accessible performance support tool formatted with a specific template. The policy that supports the guideline says the learning designer posts the templated performance support PDF on the intranet. The instructions for locating and applying the template and uploading the final support document are listed as procedures that support the policy.

Thus, if a designer does not create the performance support document for a given course, the course violates the policy, does not comply with the guideline, and ultimately does not support the standard. The same is true if the designer uses a different template, uses the appropriate template but misapplies it, or creates the document correctly but does not post it in the appropriate location. Because this standard is not met, the designer has not ensured the learner is supported beyond the structured learning experience, and the product does not meet its quality goals. Ultimately, this may put performance, and the organization, at risk.

If the challenge of creating and upholding the standard was not readily apparent to you before, it should be crystal clear now. How does the team achieve consensus on the mission or standard that supports it? Are there any exceptions? If so, what are they, and what mechanism will designers use to request an exemption? What if people do not know how to use the template? And, perhaps more importantly, what will you gain or lose by using a standard as the road map to provide value to the organization? Answering these questions is what the process of defining your standard is for.

While creating a quality management system may seem daunting, there is good news. First, you already have guidelines and use them to make design decisions, whether or not you are fully aware you're doing so. They may not be documented, entirely evidenced based, or applied consistently, but they exist. Second, while there are few concrete standards backed by consensus in our industry, there are guidelines and best practices for L&D work lurking inside the volumes of expert literature. You may also borrow guidelines from other industries. For example, you can find writing and usage guidelines in style guides. Interface design is its own discipline rich with research and best practices. The publishing industry depends on rules regarding layouts that guide readers through documents. The road to quality management is paved with standards but begins with defining the term itself.

A Brief History of Quality Management

"Quality has to be managed—it will not just happen" (Oakland, Oakland, and Turner 2021). *Quality management* is often defined as the systematic approach to ensuring that products and services meet stakeholder expectations and guidelines. Stakeholders are usually people with a vested interest in the product or service being created. For example, they could be the product's end users, like learners, or organizational leaders sponsoring the endeavor.

The history of quality management can be traced back to medieval Europe, where craftsmen organized into guilds that enforced rules for product and service quality. With the advent of the Industrial Revolution, quality management shifted from craftsmanship to factory production, where inspection and statistical methods were used to control quality. Modern quality management is framed by the people who contributed to its evolution. These experts introduced concepts, such as total quality control, zero defects, and continuous improvement.

Shewhart's Plan-Do-Check-Act (PDCA) Cycle

The origins of modern quality management can be found in early 20th century with the pioneering work of Walter A. Shewhart. His theories and techniques are still used today to identify defects, reduce variation, and improve product and service quality while reducing the costs associated with production. Shewhart proposed the plan-do-check-act (PDCA) cycle, which is a four-step quality management method used to ensure that product or service quality is continuously monitored and improved. The *plan phase* involves studying the current state, setting goals, and developing an improvement plan. The *do phase* requires implementing the plan on a small scale and collecting data to evaluate its effectiveness. During the *check phase*, you analyze the data collected during the do phase to determine if the changes have improved the quality. Finally, the *act phase* focuses on implementing the changes on a larger scale and standardizing the new process or approach.

When I first learned about PDCA, I considered its similarity to the ADDIE model. If you're unfamiliar with ADDIE, it's a process framework used in education and training. It consists of five phases: analysis (identifying learning needs), design (planning the learning experience), development (creating the learning experience), implementation (delivering the learning experience), and evaluation (assessing effectiveness). It shows how much our production work resembles other industries, so it's not a stretch to borrow from strategies used outside L&D.

Shewhart's work on statistical process control (SPC) laid the foundation for modern quality management practices. SPC is a quality management method that involves monitoring a process to identify and respond to variability in that process. SPC consists of analyzing data to determine the cause of the variation and then taking corrective action to eliminate it. PDCA and SPC are key components of modern quality management practices used in many industries worldwide.

PDCA is relevant to L&D quality processes because it can be used to determine the impact of *variation*, which, in quality management, refers to differences in a product or service that affect its overall quality. For example, even without a formal, documented quality management system, we review L&D materials against our expectations for those materials. Our expectations go beyond errors or features that do not conform to our criteria for what a workbook should look like, given its role in the learning experience. We are searching for problematic variations from our shared understanding of how a learner should be able to engage with a workbook during a workshop. And it's not just our expectations as an industry. Workshop participants also expect consistency when using workbooks.

Variations can be caused by differences in how a product is manufactured or how a service is delivered. If different designers are working on projects, variability is inevitable. The goal should not be to eradicate all variability among learning products. However, managing variation is a critical component of quality management because reducing it can lead to improved product or service quality and increased customer satisfaction. This principle makes more sense once you create products and services based on guidelines and seek to minimize outcomes that vary from them. The PDCA principles will also be reflected in the recommended methodology this book provides. Specifically, the plan phase supports the idea that quality considerations should be planned early in the design process rather than waiting to address issues after finding them following production.

The Juran Trilogy: Quality Control, Improvement, and Planning

Joseph Juran was an engineer and management consultant widely regarded as the father of modern quality management. He is credited with developing the Juran Trilogy, which includes quality planning, control, and improvement. The trilogy helps organizations ensure that their products and services meet or exceed customer requirements by focusing on the planning, control, and improvement of quality throughout the entire organization.

In learning and development, the Juran Trilogy may work like this:

- **Quality planning** involves setting clear and measurable objectives for training programs or educational courses.
- **Quality control** involves monitoring and evaluating design and development processes to ensure they align with established objectives.
- **Quality improvement** focuses on continuously enhancing programs and processes according to the data collected during quality control and making adjustments to optimize learning outcomes and efficiency.

Juran's contributions to quality management include the development of the Pareto principle, which states that a few causes are responsible for a large percentage of the problems in a process or system. It's often called the 80/20 rule because it suggests that roughly 80 percent of outcomes result from 20 percent of causes. In quality management, it's used to identify the most critical issues that need to be addressed to achieve the most significant impact on quality improvement. The Pareto principle is relevant to L&D professionals because it encourages us to avoid making assumptions about how quality is being compromised. For example, suppose you are receiving inconsistent results from a vendor. Rather than replacing that vendor, you may change your process to include a more effective way to communicate your expectations. Instead of only emailing the vendor's team the style guide and assuming they will read it, you can make the quality discussion part of your kickoff meeting and include a walk-through of the style guide. In other words, depending on the issue's root cause, a small change can make a significant impact.

Ishikawa's Fishbone Diagram

Identifying the root causes of barriers is vital to developing sustainable quality management processes. Consequently, using tools to pinpoint cause and effect is essential. Kaoru Ishikawa, an engineer and quality control expert, is known for developing the Ishikawa (fishbone or cause-and-effect) diagram (Figure 1-1). This diagram is a tool for identifying the root cause of a problem or issue and developing solutions to address it. For example, instead of making assumptions about the relationship between a designer's skill set and course errors, consider other causes, like barriers to success.

Figure 1-1. The Fishbone Diagram

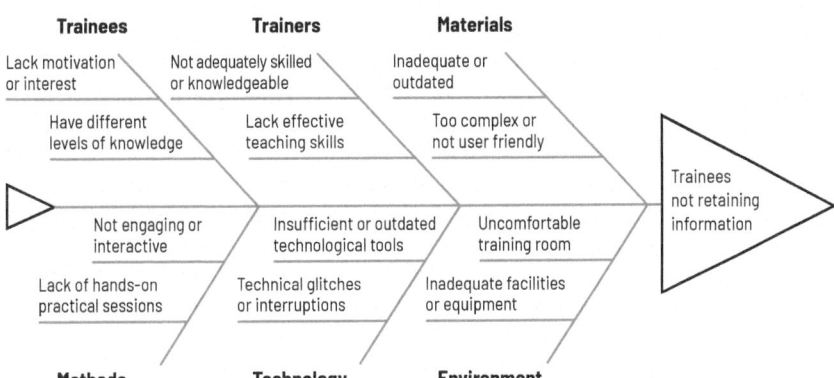

Feigenbaum's Total Quality Control

While I've focused on L&D's role in quality management, quality is the responsibility of everyone in the organization, which is the driving force behind *total quality control*. Armand Feigenbaum, an American quality control expert, is credited with developing the total quality control concept. It emphasizes the importance of quality control at every stage of the production process, from design to delivery. This approach is based on the idea that quality is not the responsibility of a single department or individual but rather it's a shared responsibility across the entire organization. In other words, you are not burdening your SMEs by including them in the review process. It's their responsibility to assess accuracy and guideline compliance.

Deming's Quality Management Contributions

The four founders I've mentioned so far are instrumental in how we approach quality management today. However, the founder whose practices align most closely with how L&D professionals engage in quality management is William Edwards Deming, a renowned American statistician, educator, and management consultant born in Sioux City, Iowa. Deming incorporated statistical methods, which are tools used to analyze data and make informed decisions.

For example, suppose completion rates for a new course are far below those of similar courses. Along with investigating other causes, an L&D professional might use statistical process control (SPC) to help identify a quality issue by continuously monitoring course completion rates, as well as control charts, which are graphical tools used in SPC to monitor the stability and performance of a process over time. In this case, one control chart displays data points for completion rates of each module or course, plotted over time. It helps you visualize trends, variations, and any data points that fall outside established control limits, signaling potential issues in course completion rates. When completion rates for a specific module consistently fall below the control limits on the chart, it indicates a problem that needs investigation and corrective action. If the module's confusing content is found to be contributing to the drop, completion rates should improve after it is revised.

Deming's statistical methods were beneficial during World War II. He later became involved with the Union of Japanese Scientists and Engineers (JUSE), where he lectured on statistical methods and modern quality principles. Deming's work was mostly unknown in the United States until an episode of the television documentary series *NBC White Paper*, "If Japan Can . . . Why Can't We?" aired in 1980. It explored the reasons behind the decline of American manufacturing and the rise of Japanese industry. It also examined the different approaches taken by both countries and suggested that the United States could learn from Japan's emphasis on quality, innovation, and continuous improvement. Deming became well known and highly regarded in the worldwide quality management community after the episode aired.

Deming's teachings encourage managers to focus on variability and understand the difference between common causes and special causes of variation in a process. *Common cause variation* is inherent in the process and results from random factors that cannot be controlled. Alternatively, *special cause variation* occurs because of specific factors that can be identified and addressed. Deming believed it was essential to distinguish between the two types of variation to effectively improve a process.

For example, suppose student engagement in an online, multisession course is fluctuating. Common cause variation in online learning might manifest as minor fluctuations in student engagement levels throughout a course; levels may naturally ebb and flow due to factors like daily routines, personal commitments, or outside distractions. These variations are typical and expected within the online learning context, and they do not necessarily indicate a significant problem with the course or its design. However, a sudden and significant decrease in course engagement represents a special cause variation because it cannot be attributed to normal fluctuations. This sudden decrease may occur due to a specific issue, such as technical problems or negative informal feedback about the course content, instructor, or the overall learning experience.

Deming's Plan-Do-Study-Act (PDSA) Cycle

Deming also encouraged organizations to adopt a systematic problem-solving approach, later known as the Deming Cycle, or the Plan-Do-Study-Act (PDSA) cycle. Shewhart's PDCA and Deming's PDSA cycles are both iterative models for continuous improvement. However, Deming's PDSA cycle emphasizes the importance of studying the results of an implemented change before acting on them, allowing for data-driven decision making and a more accurate understanding of the change's impact.

The PDSA cycle's four steps and their corresponding activities are:

- **Plan.** Define the problem and aim or intent, develop a hypothesis, set targets, and develop a suitable recommendation.
- **Do.** Implement the plan on a small scale and record, observe, and collect data.
- **Study.** Analyze the results to determine if the plan was successful.
- **Act.** If the plan was successful, implement it on a larger scale. If not, adjust the plan and repeat the cycle.

Both *study* in the PDSA cycle and *check* in the PDCA cycle involve evaluating the outcomes of the actions taken during the respective *do* phases. PDSA's *study* step is more focused on learning and gaining a deeper understanding of the process and its outcomes. It involves ongoing data collection and analysis to refine understanding. The PDCA cycle's *check* step is more focused on confirming whether the objectives were met and the actions align with the original plan—it often serves as a validation step. The choice between the two methodologies typically depends on an organization's specific needs and the desired emphasis on learning and goal achievement.

Deming's 14 Points

Deming's 1986 book, *Out of the Crisis*, is considered a seminal work in quality management. It provides a comprehensive framework for improving quality and productivity in organizations, emphasizing the importance of a systematic and integrated approach to management. Deming also introduces his famous 14 points for quality management, which is a set of management principles that provide a framework for improving the quality of products and services while increasing organizational efficiency. They also emphasize the importance of leadership, continuous improvement, eliminating barriers between departments, and employee engagement.

Reflecting on the 14 Points

Deming's 14 points are listed in Table 1-1 with corresponding reflection questions about how each point manifests in your organization. The answers to these questions facilitate understanding Deming's 14 points and begin the information gathering process.

Table 1-1. Deming's 14 Points

	Deming's Points	L&D Reflection Questions
1.	Create constancy of purpose toward improvement of product and service; aim to become competitive, stay in business, and provide jobs.	What mission or guiding philosophy supports your team's quest to design and develop high-quality products?
2.	Adopt the new philosophy. We are in a new economic age. Western management must awaken to the challenge, must learn their responsibilities, and take on leadership for change.	How does leadership demonstrate that they are ready to develop, champion, and consistently enforce a quality-first approach?
3.	Cease dependence on inspection to achieve quality. Eliminate the need for inspection on a mass basis by building quality into the product in the first place.	What is your team's approach to controlling quality throughout the design and development process, rather than solely relying on inspection at the end?
4.	End the practice of awarding business on the basis of price tag. Instead minimize total cost. Move toward a single supplier for any one item, on a long-term relationship of loyalty and trust.	How does your process for selecting vendors emphasize proof of quality over price?
5.	Improve constantly and forever the system of production and service. To improve quality and productivity, and thus constantly decrease costs.	How does your team integrate process and quality improvement discussions into your team and one-on-one meetings?
6.	Institute training on the job.	How are employees within your organization encouraged to share knowledge, collaborate, and learn in the flow of work?
7.	Institute leadership. The aim of supervision should be to help people and machines to do a better job. Supervision of management is in need of overhaul, as well as supervision of production workers.	What role does L&D leadership play in establishing and supporting design and development processes?
8.	Drive out fear, so that everyone may work effectively for the company.	How does leadership support your team's ability to communicate their concerns about design and development processes, like unrealistic deadlines?
9.	Break down barriers between departments.	How collaborative are your development and design processes when working with SMEs and stakeholders from other departments?

Table 1-1. (cont.)

	Deming's Points	L&D Reflection Questions
10.	Eliminate slogans, exhortations, and targets for the workforce asking for zero defects and new levels of productivity. Such exhortations only create adversarial relationships, as the bulk of the causes of low quality and low productivity belong to the system and thus are beyond the power of the workforce.	How does your team's leadership define productivity? What other guidelines are your team measured by?
11.	A. Eliminate work standards (quotas) on the factory floor. Substitute leadership. B. Eliminate management by objectives. Eliminate management by numbers, numerical goals. Substitute leadership.	How is productivity measured? How are designers and developers supported as they navigate the production process and meet productivity goals and deadlines?
12.	A. Remove barriers that rob the hourly worker of his right to pride of workmanship. The responsibilities of supervisors must be changed from sheer numbers to quality. B. Remove barriers that rob people in management and in engineering of their right to pride of workmanship. This means abolishment of annual or merit rating and of management by objectives.	What barriers to quality exist in your design and development processes? For each one, what steps can be taken toward removing or reducing the impact of these barriers?
13.	Institute a vigorous program of education and self-improvement.	How are the individuals on your team encouraged to improve their skills to better meet expectations?
14.	Put everybody in the company to work to accomplish the transformation. The transformation is everybody's job.	How are expectations about their roles in the design and development processes communicated to SMEs and stakeholders?

How Implementing a Quality Management System Benefits L&D

Your answers to the reflection questions in Table 1-1 may have encouraged you because your team is well on its way, or maybe they discouraged you and left you wondering if your team will ever get where you think it needs to be. If it's the latter, rest assured—while your team may not have a formalized process, there are some guardrails in place; otherwise, none of your projects would be successful—and that's unlikely. Knowing the benefits of implementing a quality management system will help galvanize your team to get started, regardless of how near you are to your destination. Frankly, only you and your team will know the benefits because you know what problems you're solving. However, most benefits will serve all L&D groups, although they may manifest differently depending on your organization's structure and production process.

Some benefits will be seen and felt sooner than others. Immediately, you should notice fewer errors in your L&D materials. Many people may think that error reduction is inconsequential, but it has far-reaching implications beyond catching missed commas. Because it leads to less time spent reworking material, a financial and resource management benefit exists for the L&D team and your organization. Fewer errors in the distributed materials also mean fewer disruptions to the learning experience.

But the real benefits go beyond finding and fixing errors. With a formalized and consistently applied quality management system, teams may:

- **Gain clarity into the design and development procedures.** Since there is no one way to design and develop instruction, practitioners have created their own procedures. It's necessary to encourage them to document these practices because adopting new practices is challenging if you do not understand existing ones.

- **Streamline existing processes and formalize new ones.** Once you know what procedures exist, it's easier to simplify or abandon them altogether. Also, formalizing processes by documenting them and adjusting timelines to accommodate their steps increases the likelihood of following them.

- **Prioritize the importance of quality policies and procedures.** Many L&D professionals have been led to believe that their profession does not exist. You may have heard comments like, "Anyone can create training. It's just PowerPoint." Or been told that our work consists of simply making presentations pretty or (my favorite) fancy. While these statements range from irritating to downright false, L&D professionals should be able to present, or at least articulate, what our processes are in simple language. Presenting quality procedures as formalized and documented steps can go a long way in notifying the rest of the organization that we mean business.

- **Provide guidelines for design teams.** It's helpful for people to understand what's expected of them and have guidelines to support those outcomes. Guidelines are based on standardization, which involves the creation of specific, universally accepted guidelines or protocols. These standardized guidelines describe criteria, procedures, or specifications that ensure consistency and quality in various processes, products, or services across industries, resulting in higher customer satisfaction and cost-effective production. But many believe that guidelines and standards can discourage creativity and innovation. Consequently, while your team may be willing to adopt quality management processes in theory, they may resist in practice because doing so will inevitably result in a loss of some control. A point that I will repeatedly make throughout this book is that no quality management system should be presented as punitive, and I encouraged you to communicate that point early and often. Also, the focus should be on the quality of the course, not the quality of the course's designer.

Throughout this book, you'll be encouraged to add to this list of benefits. Understanding how you, your team, and your organization will benefit—and being able to share that information—is an essential part of the commitment process.

CHAPTER 2
Overview of Quality Management Systems

IN THIS CHAPTER:
- Exploring the quality-first mindset
- An overview of quality management systems
- The importance of formalizing quality management systems

Many years ago, I worked for an organization that implemented a cloud-based file storage system, which was a new concept at the time. I decided the training department could use the system to create a knowledge base to store guidelines, templates, and other documentation. I mapped out my idea and started discussing it with colleagues to get their feedback on whether it was sustainable. Although this was early in my career, I had enough experience to know that good ideas have short shelf lives if the people expected to engage in them don't see the personal benefits of doing so.

Most people liked the idea and agreed that a knowledge base could help our team organize information and make it readily accessible. We had recently experienced a round of layoffs, and those who remained could only watch as years of knowledge and best practices were escorted out the door. With so many colleagues on board, I was excited to start building.

And then I asked Sharon for her opinion. Sharon was a vice president with decades of experience. She'd seen initiatives succeed and fail but always seemed optimistic about what was coming next. So, I was surprised by her sobering take on my suggestion—"Sure, it's a good idea, but I wonder whether it will end up being just another thing."

"What do you mean?" I asked, despite knowing exactly what she meant. She expressed the concern we all had but didn't share because none of us wanted to openly question the value of a central repository of knowledge.

She elaborated, saying, "I mean, I wonder whether it will just become another thing that we say we will do, not fully commit to, and then have meetings about why it failed. Then, in a few years, someone else will have the same idea, and the cycle will begin again. But that's because it's a good idea. The thing is, not all good ideas are valuable enough to be sustained."

She smiled, but all I could see was the phrase "not all good ideas are valuable enough" hanging in the air as she turned and walked away. She was right. It was hard to hear, but this lesson is valuable to those on the path to quality. Assume that everyone wants quality products. Assume that everyone wants to meet customer expectations. All L&D professionals value quality. No one sets out to create ineffective courses riddled with errors. However, wanting quality and doing what it takes to consistently ensure quality are two different things. Ensuring quality requires valuing engagement in quality processes over other competing priorities—like completing and implementing the course. Quality and completion are not mutually exclusive, but it often seems like it.

After speaking with Sharon, I realized that most people I spoke with were probably basing their opinions on what they thought life would be like when the knowledge base was deployed—a life with all the answers at their fingertips. They may not have considered the reality of building and maintaining such an extensive database—a life filled with creating and updating guidelines and protocols.

Beyond errors, it's a long road from training request to design and development, and navigating it takes skill and knowledge. The journey is riddled with decisions that will influence the solution's effectiveness once you've arrived at your destination. Without insight into the available routes, knowing which strategies to keep and which to amend to achieve better outcomes is challenging. Essentially, it's difficult to determine whether any process is working if it's not formalized and documented.

Why Should You Formalize a Quality Management System?

Your team already has a quality management system. In fact, your team may have several quality management systems that were each created and managed by different people. When I worked on an internal team, I had strategies for avoiding mistakes. I assumed everyone else did too, but we never discussed what they were or how to improve them. My colleagues may not have called them quality management systems; instead, those strategies were just baked into their jobs. So, quality management happens with or without oversight. However, having one formalized, flexible, and consistently applied system will benefit everyone involved.

Formalized systems have, at a minimum, the following characteristics:

- **They're governed by a mission or goal** that serves as the foundation for structure and decision making.
- **They're equipped with guidelines to measure against** so people know what is expected and how to comply with the mission.
- **They're informed by documented policies, processes, procedures, and terms** that support consistent workflow and communication.
- **They're designed to be scalable and flexible** enough for inevitable change and growth.
- **They're supported by tools and templates** to control quality as people navigate the process.

Formalizing the process helps you gain control of quality management, and there are three important reasons to do so:

1. Documenting the process
2. Legitimizing the process to stakeholders
3. Tracking the success and value of the process

Documenting the Process

I have routinely taken on learning design projects that involve preparing employees for an updated process. Ideally, the existing process they've been using should be well documented by the team before learning designers are brought onto the project. That way, we can use the existing process as a reference for teaching the updated version. In my experience, however, the client's current processes are often not documented or consistently followed, which makes updating them more challenging. In fact, I've had clients admit they were using training as an opportunity to document a process for the first time. In some cases, clients expect the instructional designer to help the stakeholder's team build a process from scratch in addition to designing the training program.

I'm always frustrated when teams don't document their processes because I've seen the consequences of not doing so, yet I've rarely had the opportunity to work in an L&D department with established processes, documented or otherwise. Sure, we had operations processes and procedures like course registration and project intake, but we typically focused on creating processes for others to follow when they engaged with us, rather than formalizing how we engaged with one another and the organization. We should hold ourselves to the same standards we hold for others. Because most L&D professionals understand the value of documenting processes, it should be easier to see how the benefits apply to what we do.

Documented processes are easier to:

- **Follow.** It's easier to follow a process if it's recorded in a manner that people can access when needed.
- **Implement consistently.** Processes communicated only by word-of-mouth are vulnerable to misinterpretation.
- **Train.** If a process is documented, you can share it with new hires while training them or when they need to perform a task.
- **Scale.** A small department may transform into a large department or a department of one in a flash. Documented processes are easier to modify when needed.
- **Improve.** Documented processes can be revisited and revised according to a predetermined schedule based on specific criteria.

Legitimizing the Process to Stakeholders

"Just make it pretty." "Our approach may not be as 'fancy' as you'd like, but we know the audience." "How long does it take to build an hour-long course? A week?"

You're lucky if you haven't heard comments like those before. L&D practitioners often complain to one another about how people outside (and sometimes inside) our industry do not always recognize learning design as a profession. It's as if asking clients for the information needed to create a learning experience is simply a way to hinder the training implementation for some benefit known only to us. They think our recommendations are personal preferences or opinions, rather than guidance based on research and experience.

The sentiment among L&D professionals is that others simply do not know what we do. People are often driven to discount what they do not understand. However, we are not doing ourselves any favors by inconsistently implementing processes, even informal ones, or using language that is not readily understood and valued by the business to explain what we need and why. If we use a formalized process consistently, stakeholders and SMEs may treat us more respectfully because they may better understand the crucial role consistency plays in the success of our design processes.

Tracking the Success and Value of the Process

As I previously mentioned, you already have a quality management system. Even if your courses are not completely error free by the time they make it into the learners' hands, they are functioning enough to register completion on a learning management system (LMS) or for learners to navigate during a workshop. So, your process must be working. Or is it? It's challenging enough to determine whether participants learn from our courses, let alone whether an undiscovered typo leads to a misunderstanding. Are you waiting for learners to tell you about those typos? Let's assume a learner found the error and wants to report it. Is there a mechanism for them to do so?

It's also good to know where the problems come from. Implementing quality management is not about catching people who make errors. Everyone makes errors. This is about developing strategies to identify errors during production and reduce errors in the future. But you can't track any of this without having documented processes for people to follow. This makes it easier to see exactly where a designer is challenged and then provide them the tools to improve. But this all relies on everyone understanding what is expected of them. Just remember, learning who is struggling with quality should lead to development opportunities, not a reprimand.

As Deming writes in his classic 1982 book, *Quality Productivity and Competitive Position*, "It is not enough that top management commit themselves for life to quality and productivity. They must know what it is that they are committed to—i.e., what they must do." This is true for everyone engaged in the process. And that commitment starts before review processes begin. It starts with a *mindset*—a set of attitudes and beliefs that shapes perspectives and behaviors. A person may need to shift their mindset because it influences their responses to various situations and challenges they may encounter when they're required to embrace a change.

The Engine Behind the System: The Quality-First Mindset

I had my kitchen remodeled once. I started out wanting a fantastic, state-of-the-art cooking oasis. But after eight weeks of remodelers hammering, drilling, dragging, and dropping tools and other materials, all I wanted was a finished kitchen. I know nothing about construction work, but that didn't stop me from questioning their choices and offering helpful alternatives. It wasn't that I didn't trust them, I didn't like not having control, or thought I could do a better job. The problem was I had no insight into what was happening because I didn't know how to do their job or how long it took to do it. To make matters worse, I tried to use my own logic even though it did not apply. For example, I knew the size of my kitchen, saw painting happening, and saw eight hours passing, so I figured I'd be able to walk into a fully painted kitchen at the end of the day. But I didn't know that primer goes on before the paint! I imagine that our clients experience something similar as they wait for us to complete their courses. They want a spectacular course and have a vague notion of what that looks like. But after a few weeks or so, the desire to have a completed project takes priority.

When the client engages in an L&D project, they typically have one goal: implementation. They assume that implementation consists of two parts—completion and quality. At the start of the project, completion and quality have equal footing, but once the project is underway, completion often overtakes quality to become the priority. If milestones are missed, and deadlines aren't met, stakeholders may begin referring to the course as a "band-aid solution," "the minimum viable product," or "version one"—labels the solution was not initially intended to have. Some rationalize their choices by thinking the released version will be good enough because it meets basic needs. Some silently or loudly protest, accepting that while the solution will solve nothing in its current state, they can't stop the proverbial horse from leaving the barn due to a lack of power or time. Others, typically the designers and developers, are irritated to release a less-than-ideal course, but are more than happy to move on to another project.

The problem with all three responses is that there may not actually be a standard for the course to exceed, meet, or fall short of. Sure, everyone has their idea of what quality means, but if that standard isn't agreed upon, documented, and accompanied by strategies for meeting it, how can a group of people arrive at the same place when they are heading in different directions and unclear about their own destinations?

While the first step on the path to quality is to define *quality*, there's a process that must happen before you can begin having those discussions. I've said that everyone believes they are committed to implementing high-quality products, so if you make everyone on a project assert their position on whether quality is the top priority, everyone will say yes and may find the implication that they would not prioritize quality condescending. Consequently, verbal or written declarations on the value of quality are not particularly useful. Instead, what's needed is a commitment to pursuing quality and what that journey will entail. The team (and ultimately the organization) needs to commit to the *quality-first mindset*, which is a way of thinking that focuses on creating value for the client, rather than on short-term gains or meeting superficial metrics. The quality-first mindset is about a commitment to excellence and continuous improvement.

In an L&D context, the quality-first mindset means not only designing and developing learning experiences but creating quality products and prioritizing doing so over everything else. Quality must come before all other things—including deadlines, costs, and speed. It comes before the desire to maintain the status quo. It comes before opinions about how long a process should take versus how long it actually does. It even comes before your doubts about whether quality management is possible at your organization. Shifting your mindset from *if you can implement a formal quality management system* to *how you can implement one* is the first step to adopting the mindset you need to get—and keep—everyone on board.

In practice, the quality-first mindset needs to be operationalized, meaning that strategies intended to put quality first must show up throughout the management of the team and the creation process for their products. For example, for a long time, I didn't know how many hours it took me to create a course based on its complexity, length, delivery modality, and other factors. This often led to miscalculations that compromised quality because I had to rush to meet the promised deadline. Of course, the time saved by rushing was canceled out by fixing errors found during the final review or addressing design shortcuts that proved to be bad decisions during the pilot.

My erroneous guesses were often driven by the client's need to deliver a course on a specific date, which is a fair request. They need the course on their schedule, not mine. But no one is well served by promises to make deadlines you know are impossible to meet when creating a quality course. I needed to find a way to give more accurate timeframes, but I also knew that simply telling clients that design and development would take longer than they'd like wouldn't be received well in many circumstances.

I had to take two steps to provide more accurate timelines. First, I had to find the most accurate timeframes by better tracking my design and development processes and gaining insight into the factors that affected them. Second, I had to communicate these findings to my clients so they could better understand the workflow schedule, and I needed to provide data and documentation to support my position. I soon discovered, however, that neither step was possible without first defining what quality benchmarks I intended to hit. The discussion I needed to have with clients was less about deadlines and more about our expectations of quality and how much effort and time it would take to meet those expectations. Reframing the focus from time goals to quality goals is a demonstration of the quality-first mindset.

Barriers to the Quality-First Mindset

In theory, quality is already everyone's priority because we all begin a project with the best intentions and want to design and develop an excellent learning experience. In practice, however, we often fall short of living up to the quality-first mindset's principles. There are several reasons why L&D might be challenged with this shift in approach:

- **Prioritizing the needs of the business.** L&D exists to support the business. So, if the business wants an instructor-led course delivered in two weeks, the prevailing belief is that you should answer the call. In this case, despite your best efforts, completion is the priority, and while quality is assumed, it couldn't possibly be the top priority because the short timeframe is the focus of the request. If quality was the focus, the ask would be, "Can you create an effective solution that will help us address a performance gap? Tell us all the resources you need and when delivery is possible. We will adjust our timelines and dependencies based on your dates." (Note that there's no mention of courses as the solution.) Regardless of what the stakeholders believe, L&D professionals know it's probably unrealistic to traverse the design-to-implementation spectrum in two weeks. What does this mean for you? The quality-first mindset requires you to be proactive and make a good-faith effort to find timelines that meet the need for quality and timely completion.
- **Managing a shortage of L&D resources and capabilities.** Teams may be dedicated to quality, but their good intentions are undermined

when balancing quality with other demands on their limited resources. There's often barely enough time to complete a functioning course, let alone send it through a quality management system. Practicing a quality-first mindset can be expensive in expected and unexpected ways—one of which is the cost of adding resources or somehow making time for existing resources to be redirected. The shift may require considering *what is* in addition to *what could be*. It's also important to acknowledge that people cannot comply with guidelines requiring competencies and skills they do not have. I don't recommend you attempt to teach learning design through a standard. (This challenge is explored in greater detail in chapter 6.) So, what does this mean for you? The quality-first mindset requires you to remove barriers to quality that are inherent in your team's structure and capabilities.

- **Facing a lack of leadership support.** Many L&D leaders have no background in learning design. Some even have a low opinion of the L&D function despite being responsible for leading it. I've often wondered how disengaged leaders landed leadership roles or why they accepted them. While some leaders are willing to learn, others double down on running a training department like the business they were transplanted from. Regardless, a lack of knowledge of the training function can lead to a lack of understanding of the industry's challenges when attempting to balance efficiency with effectiveness. So, what do this mean for you? As I discuss throughout this book, quality management systems can be created from the bottom up, but they are sustained from the top down. Leadership must take an active role in both building and supporting the system through every iteration.

- **Quality hasn't been defined.** It's difficult to have a quality-first mindset without a definition of quality. This challenge is explored in greater detail in chapter 4. So, what does this mean for you? The quality-first mindset is depends on you establishing a definition of quality that everyone can embrace.

Throughout this book, you can add to this list because I'll ask you to actively look for barriers and plan for the ones that exist but you didn't initially see. Ideally, you'll remove barriers or demote them to manageable risks by the end of your journey. There is no one-size-fits-all approach, so your challenges and solutions may not resemble those of other teams or organizations. The type and structure of your organization will also play a role. (I explore specific scenarios in chapter 3.)

Your Quality Management Process and Basic Terms

In this book, I use the term *quality management* to refer to the five processes needed to build a system:

1. Defining quality
2. Quality planning
3. Quality assurance
4. Quality control
5. Quality review

Each process has its own steps and requirements. This section provides an overview of the five processes, and I'll cover them in greater detail in the coming chapters. Figure 2-1 shows the inputs and output for building all five processes.

Figure 2-1. The Inputs and Outputs of a Quality Management System

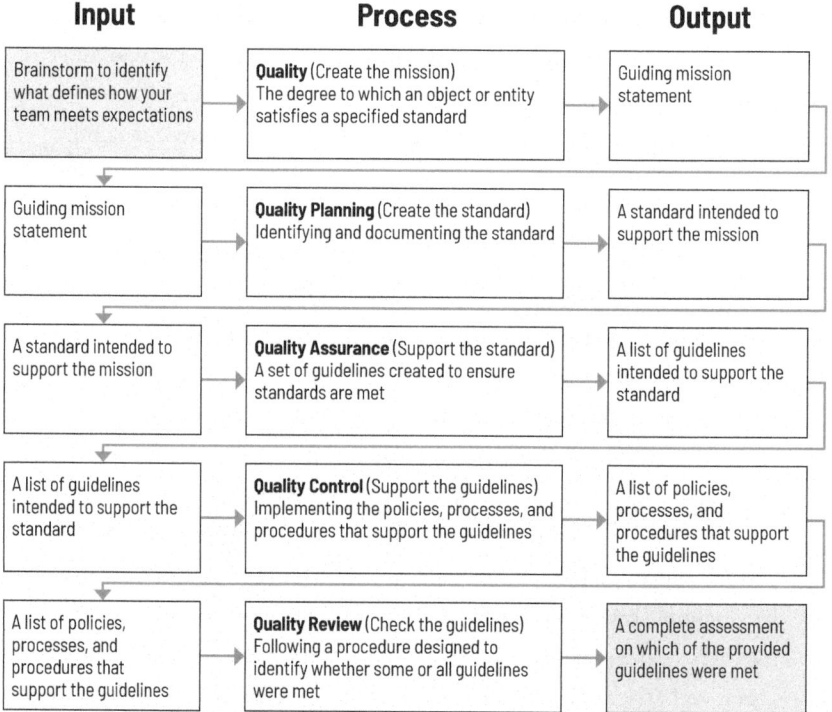

Defining Quality

Building a quality management system depends on the answer to this central question: What is quality? While this section covers the basic definition, in chapter 4, I look at strategies for identifying what quality means to your team.

ASQ suggests that *quality* is a "subjective term for which each person or sector has its own definition" (Duffy and Furterer 2020). The founders I mentioned in chapter 1 had their own definitions of quality. Deming defined it as "meeting customers' needs and wants." Juran prefers "fitness for use." Another founder, Philip Crosby—best known for developing the concept of "zero defects" by focusing on proactive prevention rather than inspection and reactive correction—focused his definition on the degree to which a product, service, or process meets established standards, specifications, regulations, or expectations, or as he put it, "conformance to requirements" (Duffy and Furterer 2020).

For the technical usage of the word, ASQ provides two meanings:
- The characteristics of a product or service that bear on its ability to satisfy stated or implied needs
- A product or service free of deficiencies

Terminology definitions are helpful when you apply them to your work to describe what quality looks like. After defining quality for your team, you can develop a mission or set of goals to support your definition. I provide guidance for completing this step and examples in chapter 4.

Quality Planning

For our purposes, *quality planning* is defined literally, so it means creating a plan to support the mission developed in the defining quality phase. While the planning stage includes expected activities like setting project goals and outlining change management strategies, the primary output of the planning stage is a standard that supports the mission. Chapter 5 and 6 include guidance for completing this process.

Quality Assurance

Quality assurance (QA) consists of guidelines designed to encourage confidence in the quality of products or services (Gravells 2016). Essentially, QA reflects the overall design of your quality management system because the guidelines describe what the products the team develops will be measured against.

The input into the QA process is the standard. The output is the guidelines that support the standard. QA is the foundation of your quality system and should be regarded as the single source of truth for what your team believes quality looks like. Guidance for completing this process is included in chapter 6.

Quality Control

Quality control (QC) is often used to describe the entire quality management system. You can find sources that will support that connection, but the following statement, taken from *Total Quality Management and Operational Excellence*, resonates: "The control of quality can only take place at the point of operation or production—where the letter is word-processed, the sales call made, the patient admitted or the chemical manufactured. The act of inspection is not quality control" (Oakland, Oakland, and Turner 2021).

QC documentation describes all the policies and procedures intended to support the guidelines included in the standard. Essentially, you cannot control the quality of a product after it is produced. So, QC is better understood as the policies and procedures employed to achieve and maintain the quality of a product, process, or service during production. It includes policies and procedures for activity but is also concerned with finding and eliminating causes of quality problems so that the standard's requirements are continually met (Oakland, Oakland, and Turner 2021).

For example, suppose one of your QA guidelines is that all courses need to have a problem-based design. The experience will focus on real-world problems that are complex and require critical thinking, collaboration, and creativity to solve. To support the guideline, you may develop a policy that requires all preliminary discussions with SMEs to focus on the problem that needs to be addressed. To support this discussion, learning designers are given a template to guide them through those initial discussions about the challenges the clients face. Using the template is a procedure that supports the policy. The template is a QC measure because you are using it to help learning designers meet the guideline to support the quality standard.

QC occurs during the design and development process, not afterward with a checklist. The QC input is the QA guidelines, and the output is the policies and procedures that support them. Guidance for completing this process is included in chapter 7.

Quality Review

ASQ defines quality inspection as "the activity of searching for errors or defects after the product or service has been created" (Duffy and Furterer 2020). *Inspection*, as defined, plays a vital role in our QM system, but instead of "quality inspection," we use "quality review" (QR) as a more accurate and familiar term for the processes conducted after the learning products are at or near completion.

During QR, we are looking for errors, but we're ultimately ensuring the learning experience complies with the guidelines set during the QA stage. The system development process typically includes creating a QR checklist for reviewers and a process for them to follow.

Quality review is often viewed as synonymous with QC. An online search for L&D QC tools will inevitably result in many checklists featuring everything you should look for when reviewing a course. But, as I've established, control needs to happen during production.

We typically focus on guidelines when creating a process and materials for reviewers to support them during the review process. As you'll see in chapter 8, you don't have to send all guidelines through review, and it's acceptable to amend the ones you do. So, review materials are often streamlined versions of the guidelines.

TIP

I recommend that you keep the detailed policies, processes, and procedures out of the review process because they may overwhelm reviewers and possibly do more harm than good. Instead, rewrite the guidelines using terminology that's more accessible to reviewers outside the L&D space.

CHAPTER 3
The Role of Quality Management in L&D

IN THIS CHAPTER:
- Quality management in an L&D context
- Gaining commitment
- Using the Getting Started worksheet

Quality management appears in many forms in learning and development. When facilitating a course or conference session on quality for L&D professionals, I like to ask for a show of hands as I read out different options for how their organizations might handle quality management. I've also conducted an online poll, which focused on the reviews, not entire quality management systems. I consider the poll unofficial due to the small sample size (139 votes) and the unverified answers. However, it still provides insight into what organizations are doing, and the results are consistent with my experience and the answers I receive when I facilitate.

Of the L&D professionals who answered my poll, nearly half (48 percent) said they conducted peer reviews, meaning their fellow designers checked their work (Figure 3-1). At 30 percent, the second-highest option was an internal dedicated team for quality management (in which "dedicated" was defined as a team that only works on quality issues for an L&D team). Next was self-review at 19 percent. Finally, only 2 percent had an external dedicated team.

Figure 3-1. Who Handles Quality Management?

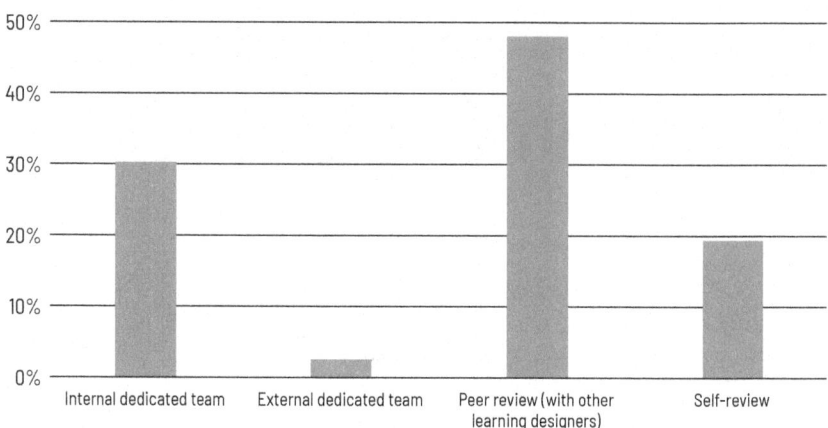

I wasn't surprised that "peer review" was the most popular response, but I was very surprised to see "internal dedicated team" come in as a close second. It's shocking to me how many people say their teams have any quality management support. And, when I ask course or session attendees in person, I can tell that others are also shocked when they look around the room at the raised hands and whisper, "What? Really?"

When I am face-to-face with respondents, I ask for elaboration. Some who first said they had a dedicated team admit that either the team consists of people who work in other roles but are good at reviews or that the team is dedicated to reviews, but they're not solely dedicated to reviewing instructional materials. Others can supply verifiable proof that they have a dedicated quality management team. But remember, these questions have historically focused on reviews, not an entire quality management system.

I once contracted with a firm that had its own dedicated quality review system. Learning designers and developers submitted review requests and materials for review to Microsoft SharePoint. The turnaround time was at least three days, during which the quality review team primarily checked for typos and inconsistencies. After completing the process, the team posted the materials with tracked changes and comments back to Microsoft SharePoint.

I'm unsure how well this process worked for others, but I struggled. After many more years of experience and studying quality processes since then, I've identified five reasons I struggled with this process:

1. **No time was allocated for quality management tasks in the timeline created and managed by the project managers.** Consequently, the initially agreed upon 10 days of development time turned into four or five days to accommodate the quality review team and any updates.

2. **Quality was only discussed at the end of the development process.** There were no official quality management processes throughout the design and development phases—one of which could have been allocating space in the timeline.

3. **There were no documented guidelines for us to adhere to, other than no typos.** If the quality review team checked for other things, no one told me about it.

4. **There was no consequence for avoiding the QC process.** While we appreciated not being admonished for skipping QC due to time, everyone may have been motivated to solve the timing issues if the stakes were higher.

5. **All the designers on this project were consultants, and there was no consideration for our varying design processes.** The client didn't prefer one design methodology over others, so we simply used our own approaches. There were no discussions regarding where and how quality management fit into our processes.

Essentially, the organization had a quality review process, but not a quality management system. I appreciated the quality review team finding typos when I could benefit from their efforts. However, just attaching proofreaders to the end of the development process is not a sound quality management strategy. In fact, this book attempts to discourage your team from jamming a quality review process onto the end of your projects and calling it QC. Doing so is tempting because it may be more than you have now, and constraints like team size, time, and other resources might mean you can't envision doing things any other way. I get that. This chapter will help you explore new ways of integrating a quality management system into your design and development workflows.

Gaining Commitment

Before I delve into some models for integrating quality management into your L&D processes, I'll start with the importance of gaining commitment for your approach to quality management. All your work building a system will be wasted if your team is not fully committed to consistently adhering to quality management guidelines. It's important to create a system that coincides with your team's level of commitment.

Chapter 2 explored the quality-first mindset and how adopting one will be useful when building a quality management system. It will also be instrumental to gaining enough commitment to sustain your project. To increase the odds of your system enjoying a long life, it should be realistic, simple, effective, and consequential. Let's take a closer look at each characteristic.

Realistic

Depending on the time and resources your team has at its disposal, be realistic about the effort that can be dedicated to quality management. For example, on paper, it may make sense for one developer to review someone else's work, but when will the reviewing developer have time to conduct a thorough review while juggling their workload? If everyone's workload remains the same, be realistic and empathic about how much time and effort people can invest in a new process.

Simple

Teams either ignore needlessly complex processes or streamline them out of existence, which means that individuals can find so many ways to adjust or circumvent a system that it loses credibility. Designing a sustainable system may require making a few tradeoffs, but a more flexible system may be better than no system at all. However, simple doesn't mean easy. *Easy* relates to the level of effort, while *simple* pertains to the absence of complexity or sophistication in a task or concept.

You'll also want to specify when to use the system. Not every course may require this type of oversight. If your system often appears to be a disproportionate response to assuring quality for a simple course, commitment will begin to wane. You'll have the opportunity to define the system's scope, which will ensure that the guidelines specify what should be included and excluded.

Effective

Determining the effectiveness of any system begins with identifying the problem the system is supposed to solve. Let's be honest—if no one sees the need for a quality management system, don't build one. People don't use what they don't value. If all your designers and developers are willing and able to shoulder the complete burden of ensuring all materials meet their chosen quality guidelines and leadership is comfortable with that, there will be little commitment to building a new system. If no learner complaints are urgent enough to drive change, you'll struggle to sustain focus on this project.

However, that may not be the case if the team either suffers in silence or has learned to make do because they have no choice. It's also possible that learners are not reporting the errors or other issues they find because they don't care (or don't remember spotting them or recognize what they see as a problem), or they may not have a mechanism to report errors back to you. There's also a chance that they have reported the errors and there's a list of them snuggled in the evaluations buried in your LMS. In addition, it's worth mentioning that just because your team believes they can create usable materials with little to no information about what's expected of them, it doesn't mean they should. How much of the time spent chasing commas could be spent creating more effective learning solutions? Also, keep in mind that we are not only talking about errors. Guidelines may cover everything from word usage to properly applied learning theories—characteristics that will take a concerted effort to locate and make an objective assessment of compliance.

Identify what issues you're trying to influence or solve and tie them to a metric. Is it the number of reported errors? Is it the time spent revising courses? Is it the time and labor involved in the design and development process? Then, determine what activities will influence that metric and how you can measure its movement. Frankly, there may be no way to truly measure it with factual data without adding considerable effort to someone's workload, so your team may have to use qualitative indicators as measures of success.

Consequential

The quality management system should be meaningful to your team so something must be gained when a team member follows the guidelines, and there should be a consequence if they don't. What are the consequences of ignoring

QA guidelines once they are in place—not just for that person but for your team and the products you create? You must define those consequences, communicate them, and most importantly, apply them consistently.

I've worked with many managers who worried about imposing consequences. They'd rather keep things as they are—if the system isn't broken, don't fix it. I argue that concept only applies when you have insight into the unbroken system. You know how everyone defines quality and effectiveness, and leadership agrees with each variation. You know what mechanisms everyone has available to assure and control quality as they define it. But, if you do not have any insights into these individual systems, how can the uncontrolled mega-system they form together be considered unbroken?

A director once told me he cared about results, and it didn't matter how they were achieved. Another said she didn't want to micromanage. These are two valid points, but I encourage you to think of this as improving systems, not people. When you have guidelines in place, the discussion shifts from the quality of a designer's skills to the degree to which they complied with a predetermined guideline. Also, as I explore in later chapters, your system can have guidelines and give people the freedom to decide how they will meet them. Always consider what you need and want to control with the understanding that it does not have to be every decision designers and developers make.

Gauging Commitment Questionnaire

You'll need to gather information about how your team members, leadership, and other stakeholders interpret the words *realistic, simple, effective,* and *consequential.* I've used a gauging commitment questionnaire to do the following:

1. **Gather data to inform the quality management system building process.** Quality management systems are collaborative, so they cannot be created in isolation. It's a mistake to create a process based only on your own experiences and then expect others to comply. They may follow along at first, but the process will always be more valuable to others if it's created with their input.

2. **Gauge interest and commitment level.** Are stakeholders enthusiastic or reluctant to provide answers to questions regarding the current quality strategies and the possibility of creating a new system? Instead of

trying to interpret their commitment, try simply asking them. Everyone will say they are committed to quality, but you need to know if they are willing engage in the potentially arduous process required to build, test, pilot, and sustain a new system that may change the way they work. This is better determined by how people make statements rather than the statements themselves.

3. **Demonstrate that you want input and are taking feedback under consideration.** Most of the answers to the questions you ask will be subjective, but still informative and valuable. As an employee, I could not determine how the learning designer in the cubicle next to mine handled quality management (in all my past experiences, designers were responsible for their own quality management), nor could I discern what their clients thought of their work. Honestly, I didn't always know how well my own work was received. All I had to go on was opinions supported by gut feelings and occasional direct or overheard conversations. What matters is that this data is meaningful to the person providing it, so treat it with respect while acknowledging that it's subjective.

You may ask the questions in the gauging commitment questionnaire using an online survey, during a focus group meeting, or in one-on-one meetings. I often do all three—I send out a survey, hold individual meetings with key stakeholders to discuss follow-up questions, and then discuss and confirm the findings during a group meeting. Table 3-1 provides an example survey with sample questions.

Table 3-1. Gauging Commitment Survey

Characteristic	Sample Questions
Realistic qualities ensure the QMS is feasible and adaptable to the organization's context.	• What resources (financial, human, and technical) can realistically be allocated to developing, implementing, and sustaining the QMS? • How could a QMS be integrated into existing processes and workflows? • How will training and support needs that may arise from implementing and sustaining the QMS be addressed? • What are the current resource constraints or barriers (budget, personnel, technology) that could affect the implementation of the QMS? • How would you prioritize the materials that should be included in the scope of the QMS? • How would you prioritize the types of projects that should be included in the scope of the QMS?

Table 3-1. (cont.)

Characteristic	Sample Questions
Simple qualities make the QMS easy to understand, use, and maintain.	• How can the system be designed for simplicity and ease of use for all stakeholders? • How can the QMS minimize bureaucracy and avoid unnecessary complexity? • What is the most straightforward strategy we can use to ensure quality? • What would discourage you from engaging in a quality management system? • How can we ensure the procedures and guidelines associated with the QMS are straightforward and easy to follow? • Does the QMS provide user-friendly navigation tools for accessing information? • What measures are in place to ensure that the system remains simple even when updates or changes are made?
Effective qualities ensure the QMS achieves its intended purpose of improving quality and performance.	• What specific quality-related goals does the QMS aim to achieve, and how are they aligned with the organization's overall objectives? • How does the QMS measure and track its progress in achieving quality goals, and how is this data used for continuous improvement? • Does the QMS provide tools and processes for identifying, analyzing, and resolving quality issues effectively? • What mechanisms are in place to review, update, and adapt the QMS to changing needs and industry standards? • How do you define quality? • How will we know that our quality management system is effective? • What mechanisms do we have to ensure compliance with set guidelines, processes, policies, and procedures?
Consequential qualities ensure the QMS contributes to long-term organizational success and sustainability.	• What consequences should someone face if they circumvent the quality management system? • How should we address noncompliance without being punitive? • How will the QMS be integrated into the organization's culture and management practices to ensure ongoing support? • How will the QMS contribute to the organization's overall competitiveness, customer satisfaction, and reputation? • What are the long-term strategic benefits of the QMS to the organization? • What are the potential risks of not implementing a QMS, and how does the proposed system mitigate these risks? • How will the success of the QMS be sustained and built upon over time?

The purpose of these questions is to drive a discussion that will help you determine whether key stakeholders understand the complexity of building and sustaining a quality management system.

What Influences How Your Quality Management System Will Look?

At this point, you may want insight into what a quality management system may look like. How these systems are built, implemented, and managed will differ based on a variety of factors, including:

- **Resources.** The more human, financial, and technical resources you have, the more system configuration choices you can make.
- **Time.** It can impact your system's implementation in three ways: First, how fast do you want to have the system in place? Second, how much time do you have to build the system given everyone's current workload? And third, how much time do you have in your existing workflows to potentially add new processes? Time limitations typically require a preplanned phased approach.
- **Leadership support.** As I'll continue to emphasize throughout this book, leadership support is crucial at every phase of the system's life cycle. For example, leadership can help your team prioritize the system's implementation and sustainability by supporting your ability to push back on competing requests for their time.
- **Team characteristics.** The size, organization, locations, and relationship complexity of the L&D function will also affect how the system is developed and managed. For example, gaining consensus on the mission and its supporting guidelines may be challenging if a team is decentralized with complex and layered reporting relationships.

While I'd need intimate insights into your organization to share perspectives on what your system should look like, I can add context to my recommended strategies by integrating a case study throughout the book.

Case Study: McCarthan Enterprises

The following sections introduce a case study featuring Asia, an L&D manager at McCarthan Enterprises. This case study provides background for the examples that appear throughout the book.

About McCarthan Enterprises

James McCarthan founded McCarthan Convenience Stores 25 years ago. Under his leadership, the company expanded to 35 locations across the United States.

After McCarthan retired five years ago, his daughter Isabella McCarthan Lopez took over the company, changed the name to McCarthan Enterprises and acquired two additional businesses, naming them McCarthan Outlets and McCarthan Wholesale Goods and Services. There are approximately 10,000 employees across the three businesses that make up McCarthan Enterprises.

Meet Asia

Asia was promoted to L&D manager after two years as a regional manager for McCarthan Convenience Stores. As a regional manager, she played a prominent role in developing training for different sites by serving as a primary SME. The experience inspired her to switch to a career in training. After earning a graduate degree in instructional design and technology three years ago, she applied and was hired for a training management position left open when the previous manager retired.

While she has some experience with learning design from a SME's perspective and a graduate degree in the field, Asia considers herself an L&D novice. She believes her company and retail knowledge effectively supports her team's L&D experience and education. Throughout her tenure as a SME, Asia built good relationships with the learning experience design team specifically. Many team members commented on how easy she was to work with compared to other SMEs in the organization.

The Learning and Development Team

The L&D function at McCarthan currently consists of 29 people (Figure 3-2). There are four teams, each with a team lead:

- **The learning experience design team** is responsible for designing and developing the learning experiences for McCarthan. All team members design and develop their assigned courses. Now that the demand for online learning has rapidly and dramatically increased, there have been discussions around splitting the design and development function based on each member's strengths. However, two experiments with the new configuration were abandoned due to workload and what Asia suspected was resistance to the change by some prominent team members.

- **The L&D business partners** serve as consultants who liaise between the L&D team and the business lines. The lead also manages the training coordinators and the project managers—a once temporary arrangement that became permanent a year ago. The results of the change have been mixed because the lead says she doesn't have enough time to manage three different functions.

- **The learning technology team** sources and supports the technology that the team uses. Three team members focus primarily on managing the LMS. They are considering switching to a new LMS (the third change in five years) and are currently identifying and testing different options. They are also asked to help the learning experience design team support any technology they use to develop online courses.

- **The facilitation team** delivers instructor-led training in person nationwide and online. Facilitators also conduct one-on-one and small-group training at retail sites and warehouses. Most of the team works remotely and is assigned to different regions. Approximately 50 percent of the training at McCarthan is instructor-led and delivered by the facilitation team.

Figure 3-2. McCarthan's L&D Function Org Chart

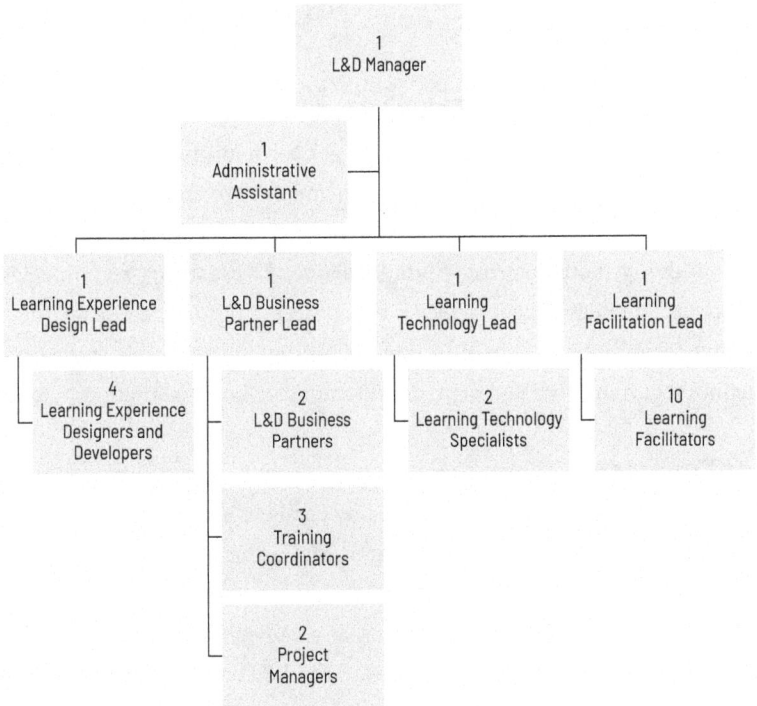

What Does Leadership Think of What the L&D Team Produces?

The solutions produced by the L&D team receive mixed reviews. Corporate training is viewed as effective and engaging, especially the corporate management curriculum. However, retail training is often not received well by business leaders. Regional and site managers complain about the quality of the training content and say it does not prepare people to do their jobs or support growth throughout their careers at McCarthan. Site leadership was enthusiastic about Asia—one of their own—taking over the training function. Unfortunately, over the last three years, very little progress has been made in winning the retail business over. They remain largely unsatisfied with the speed of delivery and the quality of the solution once they receive it.

What Does the L&D Team Think?

The L&D team also has complaints. They get constant pushback from business leaders on everything from designs to implementation strategies. The learning experience design lead, Jabari, believes that a lack of consistent guidelines and everyone "doing their own thing" are to blame. The learning technologies and business partner teams have policies and procedures for their team functions regarding technology, intake, and scheduling, but they haven't agreed on any guidelines regarding course design, development, or implementation.

Asia's Challenge

Asia wants to get control of the situation and change the narrative about the value of the L&D team and their contributions to McCarthan Enterprises. She and her team also want to improve the quality of the learning experiences they produce.

After meeting with her team and company leadership, they agree that the best approach would be to develop guidelines so the L&D team knows what they are expected to deliver and the business knows what they will receive. Stakeholders will also better understand their roles in the solution development process. They hope collaborating on building and engaging in a quality management system will open communication and get everyone on the same page.

But where do they begin to build a quality management system? I'll use Asia's challenge to add context to examples in the book, but everyone's situation is different. I encourage you to use your organization as the primary reference point.

The Getting Started Worksheet

What is the state of quality management in your organization? While you have your own ideas, you won't know until you look around. The Getting Started worksheet can help with that. It's intended to get you thinking about how you may approach building your processes. Keep in mind that the questions and answers focus on the process of developing the quality management system—not the system itself. For example, the project manager supporting the development of the system may not engage with the system after it's built.

I've used this worksheet with clients as a way to help them answer the following questions:

- What model are you currently using to manage quality?
- What issues are you addressing by implementing a quality management system, and what's driving the need to address them now?
- Who will be involved in the design of the quality management system, and what role will they play?
- What is the timeframe for implementing the system and what's driving it?
- What potential resistance and barriers do you expect?
- What project and communication tools do you hope to use throughout the quality management system's development process? If the tools are online, can you ensure everyone has access?
- What types of materials do you plan to create quality processes for?

The process I follow in this book includes the research needed to find the answers to these questions. Consequently, you do not need all the answers now, but try to answer as many as you can to the best of your ability.

The Getting Started worksheet is both an information gathering tool and a reflection tool. You will use the information recorded on the sheet to inform your next step, which is defining quality. Please take a moment to review Asia's completed Getting Started Worksheet in the appendix. You'll also find a blank version that you can use.

Your Thoughts

After reviewing Asia's completed worksheet, take a moment to consider the following prompts and write down your thoughts.

1. How are Asia's answers similar to yours?

2. What else would you ask Asia?

3. What other barriers do you imagine Asia's team may encounter?

CHAPTER 4
Defining Quality for Your Team

IN THIS CHAPTER:
- Identifying what quality means
- Assessing the current state
- Writing a mission statement

During my time as an internal learning designer, we used terms like *accurate*, *good*, *engaging*, and *effective* to discuss the quality of a learning experience. The word *quality* was only used when referring to reviews, which some called *quality control* or *quality check*. The quality review measures were usually focused on accuracy, but accuracy does not necessarily mean quality. A course could be 100 percent accurate but fail to engage the learner or lead to the desired behavior change. And yet, it often seems as if accuracy is where the quality discussion begins and ends.

Chapter 3 provided insight into the training function at McCarthan Enterprises. Asia completed the Getting Started worksheet, which gave her a clearer idea of where she and her team stand. She also explored strategies for gaining commitment from the project team, which is an essential early step in starting and sustaining the project. Now, she's ready—and you're ready—to tackle the big overarching question: "What is quality?"

What Is Quality?

If you search the web for the phrase "training quality assurance" or some variation of it, your results will be filled with checklists intended to help you pick apart a course to find errors. But, after all the design and development work you did to create a course, why are you just now introducing a set of criteria to retroactively check for? What if you started the design and development process with the checklist, using it as a guide to support you as you build the course? And what if that checklist was designed to support a significant vision about more than just accuracy? What if, before you got to the checklist of retroactive review questions, you could reference a comprehensive list of statements explaining the criteria for quality to refer to as you build the course?

A proactive approach to quality requires knowing the destination before you start the journey. It starts with answering the overarching question: "What is quality?" Everything your team does after this point serves to address that question, and this chapter will help you find your answer.

Defining Quality

Course design and development processes are already, or should be, in place. They should have checks and balances to ensure that they are successfully completed. Some may see quality management as a bumper stuck to the back of development. A quality-first mindset requires viewing quality management as interwoven into the fabric of design itself. While the L&D team is not solely responsible for quality, it takes the lead in supporting an environment where quality thrives.

As I mentioned in chapter 1, ASQ defines *quality* as a "subjective term for which each person or sector has its own definition" (Duffy and Furterer 2020). However, your organization must reach a consensus on what quality means, because every process and procedure you create will be designed to support that definition.

Once quality is defined, your goal is to keep the definition stabilized. Resist the urge to change it frequently—mold the system you create to support the definition instead of changing the definition to support your system. However, if you later realize that the definition isn't serving your purposes, change it as needed—and the sooner you change it, the better. Ultimately, your definition should be broad yet specific enough to help the team define the mission, which is the next step in the process.

What Quality Means to You

Let's try an experiment. Take out a sheet of paper and follow these prompts:

1. **Write down your definition of quality.** You aren't defining what quality looks like yet. You are defining the word itself. For example, don't list the characteristics of the ideal course—instead, think about what ideal means.

2. **Ask others for their definition of quality.** Ask at least two colleagues who will be engaged in your team's quality management process to send you their definition of quality.

3. **Compare your definitions.** Write down how similar or different your definitions are.

The key is not that they are different; it's how they differ. That difference indicates how challenging it will be to arrive at a consensus—that is, if you didn't know already. What's the focus of each definition? Do they prioritize the organization or the learner? Efficiency or effectiveness? Completion or performance?

When I've discussed quality with L&D professionals, the answers are usually focused on materials and their accuracy. When differences do emerge, they center on the idea of perfection. I've seen people blurt out perfection as a knee-jerk response, but once they hear themselves say it, they quickly change their answers to something more realistic. The change probably occurs because they know perfection is subjective and they'll likely be asked follow-up questions they'd rather not answer. While discussing perfection during one of my quality management workshops, a participant said, "Who says it has to be perfect?" Who, indeed? Let's talk about several definitions of quality.

Understanding Stated or Implied Needs

As I mentioned in chapter 2, the ASQ provides two definitions for quality. Their first definition, "The characteristics of a product or service that bear on its ability to satisfy stated or implied needs," suggests that *stated* or *implied needs* must be explicitly defined and documented (Duffy and Furterer 2020). The phrase "ability to satisfy" indicates that these needs must be measurable so that a product can be compared against them to determine whether it meets the set criteria.

A *need* is the reason why people engage in a learning experience. It's a multi-faceted concept. First, the course needs to help learners meet the intended performance objectives, which are determined by the course's content and the learning design approach. Based on your experience designing and developing learning products, you've likely encountered this need many times and understand the challenges of both meeting it and knowing that you've done so. Is it possible to create a course of exceptional quality that does not lead to a shift in learning or performance? Some would argue that if a course doesn't meet a need, it's not a quality course because the need is why the course exists. However, many factors influence whether a learner who engages in a course will make a change in performance, and completing the course is only one of them. Likewise, is it possible to create the course that isn't visually appealing or academically sound but still satisfies learners' needs? A course may be hard on the eyes, but it can still serve its purpose. These are questions you'll have to answer because they force you to commit to definitions of *need* and *quality* when you and your team decide on what's being measured.

Another component of satisfying a need is whether the learner can complete the course without hindrance. Consequently, the developer must be knowledgeable and experienced with either the technology used to ensure the course is functional or, in the case of documents, that course materials are formatted to be usable and easy to navigate. The learner must also have a positive experience while engaging in the course to satisfy a need, so you and your team should not only understand what an engaging, interactive, and aesthetically pleasing experience is, but also have the skills to use all the tools at your disposal to create it. Finally, the course must satisfy a need by supplying the knowledge, practice, and reflection often necessary to shift performance.

Each facet of satisfying a need requires a different skill set that designers and developers are expected to have, but there's no universal standard for measuring competency in these skills. This is a challenge when defining needs and devising a strategy to meet them. Nevertheless, identifying and satisfying a need is crucial to defining quality.

Does "Free of Deficiencies" Mean Perfect?

ASQ's second definition of quality ("a product or service free of deficiencies") is more familiar, but there's a catch (Duffy and Furterer 2020). Which definition of *free of deficiencies* do you think is the most accurate?

- A perfect course
- A course that is error free
- A course that meets guidelines for accuracy and completion

Any of these answers could lead to an exhausting string of clarifying questions that potentially loop back to one another. For example, what does *perfect* mean? If it means free of deficiencies, what does *free of deficiencies* mean? The answer to that question is often perfect! You get the point.

To avoid confusion regarding what perfection looks like, remove it from your quality management vocabulary now. Communicate to your system development team that you are not entertaining perfection as a goal because it cannot be achieved without corresponding guidelines. In other words, chasing perfection will make it necessary to do everything possible to create and support policies and procedures that ensure designers and developers can meet those guidelines. Those are tall orders for any L&D team's leadership.

As for error free, we all agree that typos qualify as errors, so it's acceptable to say a course should be free of typos. It's a guideline that may even be measurable if errors are counted and documented in some or all courses (although that's a laborious practice I do not recommend). However, beyond accurately using "its" and "it's," you'll need to wade through a plethora of alternative spellings, varying interpretations of concise writing, and debates over comma usage. So, the question is, error free according to whom?

How you personally define *free of deficiencies* is your decision. But, if you want to create a repeatable, scalable, and documented process that others can follow, then "meets standards for accuracy and completion," is the most practical definition to adopt. So, abandon your search for perfection and instead focus on developing achievable guidelines and strategies to meet them.

Meeting Customer Standards

ASQ's first definition of quality includes the phrase "ability to satisfy stated or implied needs." Again, whose needs? Practitioners in most L&D disciplines serve many constituents. While our primary concern should be the learners' needs, many other groups also have needs that performance solutions must address.

For example, customers outside the L&D world must have also have their needs met. In *Total Quality Management and Operational Excellence*, Oakland, Oakland, and Turner (2021) say, "Quality . . . is simply meeting the customer requirements." They add, "It is important to realize that the 'meeting the customer requirements' definition of quality is not restrictive to the functional characteristics of products or services," and that "the quality of some of the products they purchase is more associated with satisfaction in ownership than some functional property." This observation is consistent with our desire as designers to provide both a working product and a satisfying experience.

There is a question that undergirds the pressure to balance efficiency with effectiveness. Who is the customer? The organization or the learner? Ideally, both are customers with different needs but the same goal. While everyone involved wants to create an effective learning experience that shifts performance, often circumstances, choices, and behaviors demonstrate that efficiency is prioritized over effectiveness.

The Process of Defining Quality

There's no one way to reach a consensus on the definition of quality. Every designer, team, and organization is different. This section provides guidance to lead you in finding your own strategy.

Where Should You Start When Defining Quality?

Let's begin with the end in mind. Here are some additional definitions of quality that you can use as a starting point to frame your thoughts and discussions:

- The degree to which a product, service, or process is consistent and reliable
- The ability of a product, service, or process to meet its intended purpose or function
- The satisfaction or value a customer or user derives from a product, service, or process
- The effectiveness and efficiency of a product, service, or process in achieving its goals
- The adherence to standards, regulations, or best practices in the design, production, or delivery of a product, service, or process

These definitions are intentionally not specific to learning and development because an important part of this journey is being able to view what we create as products and services rather than just course materials. But, if you're thinking, "Can we use one of those definitions?" then this section is for you.

4 Steps to Defining Quality

The process of defining a term and reaching consensus on that definition includes at least four steps that are not unique to any circumstance or industry:

1. Find an initial definition.
2. Prepare for a working meeting.
3. Facilitate a working meeting to reach consensus.
4. Record and confirm the definition.

These steps could be used for any situation in which a consensus needs to be met. We are simply applying this common process to defining quality.

Whether it takes a week or a year to complete all four steps depends on how far your organization is from an agreed-upon definition and its commitment to arriving at one.

Step 1. Find an Initial Definition

There are two methods for completing the first step:

1. **Shape an existing definition.** Find a definition that you believe is close to defining quality for your organization.
2. **Conduct research.** Work with your team and other stakeholders to conduct research within your organization and arrive at a definition based on your findings.

Of course, you can combine strategies or do something different. The output of this first step is to draft a definition you can bring to a working meeting. Let's discuss each method in more detail.

Method 1. Shape an Existing Definition

Find a definition similar to what you believe the final one could be. There are many sources to draw from. By this point in the book, you've learned about how the quality management founders defined the term, explored ASQ's definitions, and read additional definitions. The definitions are typically based on:

- **Customer satisfaction**—meaning the quest for quality begins with identifying what customers want and ends by satisfying that need, which typically requires a high-quality product or service that should meet a high standard in many areas (such as form, features, fit and finish, reliability, and usability). In an L&D context, you must first define who the customer is. If you decide it's the learner, then you're targeting how satisfied they are with the products your team creates. If it's the organization, the metric may be how satisfied leadership is with what your team produces. Remember, satisfying the learner and the organization are not mutually exclusive goals. What differs is how they're measured.
- **Outcomes**—meaning it's based on whether what your team is producing is leading to desired results. In an L&D context, this information could likely be culled from Kirkpatrick's Level 3 (performance) and 4 (return on expectations) evaluations.

These two types of definitions are not mutually exclusive either. After all, it's hard to imagine that training reviled by the learners could still lead to an outstanding performance. You're also unlikely to call training that is championed by learners and leadership, yet does nothing to support the organization, a quality learning experience. All you're focusing on now is what will be at the center of the definition you select.

Method 2. Conduct Research

Conducting research can help you find the gap between the current and desired states. You'll arrive at a working definition of quality by exploring your current offerings, determining where they fall short, and then clarifying your desired state based on your findings. The desired state embodies what you define as quality. Contrast this method with the first, in which you start with a common definition (the desired state) and assume there is some distance between the definition and your current state.

Method two can be conducted as a needs assessment or research project. Here's a standard list of tasks to get you started:

1. **Create a plan.** Consider how you will conduct this research, what conclusions you want to draw, and how you will gather, analyze, and use the data.

2. **Identify and categorize what data you're looking for.** For example, perhaps there are three primary categories:
   - *Experience*—quality of the course design and all other parts of the learning experience
   - *Materials*—quality of the materials that support the course design
   - *Impact*—quality of the effectiveness of the learning experience

3. **Develop criteria for each category.** For example, criteria for the materials category for an e-learning course could be typos and navigation errors and how well the materials support the overall learning experience. You are looking for problems that could have been discovered before the release but were not.

4. **Develop a strategy for recording the errors.** You have several choices, but your strategy heavily depends on what you plan to do with the data. For example, one option is to count the number of errors. But, how does determining that "Compliance course A has 10 typos" inform

your quality management process? Another option is to inventory the errors, recording what and where they are. This is an effective approach because you may find patterns among the errors, which will help you be more targeted. This information can also be used to fix or update courses. However, no matter how many courses you review, this will be a labor-intensive process. Choose a strategy that works best for your team and the data you can collect because you may not always have access to the data that is most useful. Be intentional about the type and number of items you choose to include in this initial review. For example, you may choose one course per designer or one course per curriculum or business line.

5. **Determine what the data is saying.** In the plan you created during step one, you should have described your goals and how to analyze data. This is when you put that plan into action.

6. **Prepare your working definitions of quality.** Based on your findings, write down your initial definition of quality.

TIP

The validity of any research can be compromised by bias; searching for representations of what quality is and isn't is no exception. In fact, one goal of quality management is to reduce the impact of bias on your products. I encourage you to expand your data analytics knowledge and be open to the possibility of biases intruding on your data collection and interpretation strategies.

Notes About the Initial Definition

Here are some additional notes to keep in mind before you move on to the next step:

- It's tempting to determine that quality means "meets standards." That is accurate, but not particularly useful because your definition should help you identify a standard.
- Every word you add to the definition needs to be explained somewhere. If you include the word "needs," it should be defined.

- Balance realism with optimism when developing what will serve as your team's ultimate goal. Leadership must support the team throughout their pursuit of quality, so ensure the definition of quality reflects their commitment.

Step 2. Prepare for a Working Meeting

The next step is to draft the definition and gain consensus at the working meeting. Despite the hard work you put into the draft, its essential to balance confidence in your assessment with being open to feedback.

Here are some things to do to prepare for the working meeting:
- Have at least two alternative definitions of quality, as well as rationales for each.
- Identify the goal of the meeting, which is typically to shape a definition for quality that will guide the building of the quality management system.

In addition, assign the following roles to help ensure a productive meeting:
- **Facilitator.** Helps set the agenda, guides the meeting, and ensures it stays on track.
- **Timekeeper.** Keeps track of time, per the agenda, during the meeting.
- **Recorder or note taker.** Takes notes during the meeting and summaries key points, decisions, and action items for later distribution.
- **Designated expert or resource person or people (optional).** Comes prepared with ready access to all the reference material used to help with decision making. They can also gather all the follow-up questions and find and distribute answers after the meeting. This way, the meeting won't be derailed by critical participants (such as the facilitator) needing to look up information during the meeting.

TIP

Having ready access to data and information that supports your suggested definitions is crucial. You do not want to give the impression that you're making arbitrary changes based on preferences. You are there to decide which definition is the most acceptable and valuable to your system development process.

Be intentional about who you invite to the meeting. This is a working session—everyone's opinions should be considered so who's in the room matters. You can develop your own criteria for participation, but the primary criterion is that every role in a potential quality management system should be represented, including designers, developers, reviewers, and approvers.

Decide how productive it would be to discuss the working definitions with people before the meeting so that everyone isn't hearing your recommendations for the first time. Strategies include:

- Meet one-on-one with key stakeholders, write down a definition consistent with what you heard, and then use the working meeting to confirm your interpretation.
- Work with a small team to draft the definition, and then meet with the larger group to get their input.

TIP

Send as much information as possible to participants before the meeting so they can be prepared to make some preliminary decisions. I also recommend explaining the desired outcome and what you need from them to achieve it.

Step 3. Facilitate a Team Discussion to Reach Consensus

Step 3 is to facilitate the discussion that should lead to consensus on how the team will define quality going forward. Gaining agreement from all participants is essential for effective decision making.

Here are the critical steps for gaining consensus in a meeting:

1. **Communicate the goal** by clearly defining the objective and expectations of the meeting so that all participants understand them.
2. **Demonstrate active listening** by encouraging all participants to share their thoughts and ideas and listening carefully to what they say. Then, ask clarifying questions if needed.
3. **Identify and note areas of agreement** among the participants.
4. **Identify and note areas of disagreement** among the participants. Then, take time to explore these points and attempt to find common ground.

5. **Engage in brainstorming** to find solutions to the problem, writing down all suggestions, no matter how small.
6. **Evaluate suggestions** and discuss their advantages and disadvantages to narrow the options to the most viable solutions.
7. **Vote** on the most viable solutions. Continue the discussion until a consensus is reached if there is no clear majority.
8. **Document the decision** along with reasons for it and the next steps.

In my experience, reaching a consensus on a single definition is challenging. I've been in many meetings where participants agreed to participate, but once things got started, they expressed discomfort with being responsible for making such a high-stakes decision. There can be so much deflecting, delaying, and dodging that facilitators are often tempted to let everyone off the hook and move on to the next step without a definition.

I suggest you assure your team that the definition will evolve throughout the system development process, but careful consideration must be taken for every change. So, while what is developed during the meeting is not set in stone, it will serve as a launching point for all future activities and set the tone for the entire project.

Step 4. Record and Confirm the Definition

Document the decision and email it to all participants to confirm that the definition of quality is what the team agreed to. Of course, some could take this final step as an opportunity to reopen the discussion. This is more likely to happen if the meeting didn't go as smoothly as planned, or a participant thinks that no consensus was met. You must stand firm, but this is also not something you can force through. During the planning step, prepare for the possibility of pushback and dissent.

McCarthan's Quality Definition

Returning to the case study, let's use Asia's experience at McCarthan Enterprises to add context. Asia decided to take an existing definition of quality and modify it based on input from her team. She chose this route because she understood the issues from her experience working in the field and with the L&D team. Also, in her Getting Started worksheet, she answered the question, "What issues are you addressing by implementing a quality management system?" with the following responses:

- The business and learners are complaining about the quality of the courses.
- The training team doesn't know what expectations they need to meet.
- The business leaders want a voice in the training process and want to know what to expect from the training team.

> McCarthan's L&D team defined quality as, "The degree to which a product supports the organization's performance through learning and development."

The team provided the following rationale for their definition:
- Error-ridden and nonfunctional learning products inherently do not support the organization, so the definition implies that the materials will be correct instead of explicitly stating it.
- The team wanted to indicate that they have limitations on supporting the organization, so they specified that their support comes only through L&D initiatives.
- Supporting performance requires meeting expectations in all reviews, including content, design, and technical.
- The business's primary complaint was that the team did not produce training material supporting their efforts in the retail business. Conversely, the L&D team thought they could not use their knowledge of learning design to support the organization, primarily due to a lack of trust. They all hope staying focused on this definition reinforces their common goal—the organization's performance.

The team will need to resolve one issue with their chosen definition. At some point, they will need to describe what it looks like to support the organization through learning and development.

Using the Definition to Create a Mission

Clarifying your definition of quality has a bigger purpose. You will use it to create a mission to support the quality management system. Generally, a *mission statement* is a short, concise statement that explains the purpose and goals of your quality management system. It's a tool to help guide decision making and inspire everyone engaged in creating and supporting the quality management system.

A mission statement explains why the system exists, identifies the core values guiding it, and reflects the specific goals and objectives the team wants to achieve. It's also short, memorable, and inspiring enough to get people on board and keep them there for the long haul.

It sounds like a tall order, and it is. However, crafting a mission statement is easier if you've done the work to define quality. Essentially, you're operationalizing the definition of quality—moving it from words to action.

For context, here are some examples of mission statements for quality management systems:

- To deliver a high-quality product on time and within budget, while maintaining open communication and collaboration with stakeholders
- To provide exceptional service and support to our clients, and to continuously improve our processes and offerings
- To foster a culture of learning and growth, and to empower team members to take ownership of their work and contribute to the project's success

NOTE

This process is not intended to result in a mission for the L&D function. The mission statement will just support your quality management system. However, it may be very similar to your function's overall mission.

Anatomy of a Mission Statement

Mission statements should contain the following elements:

- An explanation of the system's purpose and goals
- A definition of the system's scope and constraints
- Specific objectives or outcomes the system aims to achieve
- Values or principles that guide the system's approach or decision-making process
- Concise, memorable, and inspiring language that captures the system's purpose

You can use these elements to compose your team's quality management mission statement. Let's use Asia's team as an example. They decided that their definition of quality would be, "The degree to which a product supports the organization's performance through learning and development." Based on what she learned from going through the quality definition process, Asia used the mission elements to help her identify what to include in her mission statement (Table 4-1).

Table 4-1. Asia's Mission Statement Elements

Mission Element	Asia's Feedback
Explanation of the system's purpose and goals	To ensure targeted (not all—per our discretion) training materials flow through a quality management system to achieve the outcome
Definition of the system's scope and constraints	Only training materials created and managed by the L&D team
Specific objectives or outcomes the system aims to achieve	To release products that support the organization's performance
Values or principles that guide the system's approach or decision-making process	Collaborate to make choices that support the organization's performance
Concise, memorable, and inspiring language that captures the system's purpose	Emphasize that we all have the same goal

Asia used the mission elements and her team's definition of quality to draft the following mission statement: "To ensure targeted training materials created and managed by the L&D team support the organization's performance through learning and development with the collaborative participation of McCarthan Enterprises' leadership."

CHAPTER 5
Planning for Quality Management

IN THIS CHAPTER:
- Building a project plan for creating a quality management system
- Assembling and guiding the planning team
- Identifying and mitigating risks

Learning design is often project-based, so planning has always played a significant role in my career. Even if a project manager is assigned to my project, I provide information about the status of my work, which influences the entire project's status. The learning designer's work often requires flexibility, so requirements, strategies, and dates shift throughout a project's life cycle. While it's great to have a stable plan in place so you can focus on other priorities, that's often not the case. We find ourselves, per my favorite saying, changing the tires while the car is moving. Assuming you continue to do other work while building your quality management system, you'll essentially be planning an entire highway system while still navigating the back roads daily.

Whenever I have to balance working on a process and working within it, I am reminded of the power of planning. As an L&D manager often tasked with taking over new teams or established teams with no processes, I had little opportunity to slam on the breaks and allocate time to figuring out what we were doing and whether there were more effective strategies for doing it. As a business owner, I confront the same issues. There is simply too much competition for my time, so I'm tempted to let things continue as they are and put out fires as they flare up. But, if you spend too much time putting out fires, there will be no time left to develop strategies for preventing them. Planning for how you and your team will tackle building a new system while still working within the current, perhaps less efficient one, should happen early in the development process.

Planning might be the most critical tool in a quality management toolbox but it can also be overwhelming because "planning while working" leads many teams to scale back or not move forward with development. However, you can simplify planning for quality by having clear goals and building a plan to support only those goals. Clarity helps the team balance optimism and realism to build a plan that will work for them and not against them.

At its core, building a quality management plan is a logistics exercise that requires skill, organizational knowledge, time, and patience. As with any other plan, it's essential to identify the tools needed to communicate, track, and manage progress against expectations. You must establish and adhere to a time-line because internal projects that are perceived as supporting only the L&D function often drop in priority due to competing client needs. The value the organization places on your efforts will not exceed the value placed on the L&D function. I have found that L&D leadership has to protect the project and people working within it from both internal and external forces. For example, one manager I interviewed said that their quality management system development project was initially treated as an add-on project that people engaged in when they had time—which was rare. She had to change her approach and ensure that the project had the same standing as any other project by giving it a project manager, plan, and resources.

This chapter explores creating a project plan for building a quality management system.

The Project Plan

An early step in the quality management system development process is to build a project plan that balances details with simplicity. The more streamlined the project plan, the more likely it is to produce a sustainable result. The time spent on building a quality management system is an investment in the future of the L&D function.

While the team's usual approach to project management will likely suffice, this chapter explores the information a typical project plan includes, along with information specific to creating quality processes.

This section covers the following components of a project plan for building a process: goals and objectives, project scope, project deliverables, project timeline, roles and responsibilities, risk management, budget, and communication plan.

NOTE

You can find a project plan template in the appendix.

Goals and Objectives

The *goals and objectives section* of a project plan describe the project's purpose and what it will achieve. Your first planning step is to write a goal or objective statement. Remember that this project is not for quality management itself. Instead, you'll use the plan to develop a quality management system. In other words, this project will not result in quality learning and development materials. Rather, it will result in a quality management system. It's an important distinction because you should not set the expectation that the work will be done when this project ends. This project will ultimately describe what the work will be—how a quality management system's processes will be integrated into your analysis, design, development, implementation, and evaluation cycles.

For example, in chapter 4, Asia and her team developed an overall mission for quality management: "To ensure targeted training materials created and managed by the L&D team support the organization's performance through learning and development with the collaborative participation of McCarthan Enterprises' leadership."

The project's *goal*, and the focus of this chapter, is to build a system that will support the L&D team in achieving that mission.

Here are four examples of objective statements for planning a project intended to build a quality management system:

1. To establish a quality management system that ensures compliance with industry standards and customer requirements while reducing defects and improving overall product quality.
2. To develop a comprehensive quality management system that promotes continuous improvement and empowers employees to take ownership of the quality of their work.

3. To create a quality management framework that enables effective communication and collaboration across departments and supports a culture of quality throughout the organization.
4. To identify and document key quality indicators and develop a data-driven approach to monitor and improve quality performance.

Remember that the *quality mission* focuses on using the quality management system. The project goal focuses on developing the quality management system.

> To support their quality management mission statement, Asia's team developed a project goal statement: "To develop a comprehensive and flexible quality management system that ensures all training materials created and managed by the learning and development team meet standards for accuracy and effectiveness to support employee performance."

The two statements are related—the team's project goal supports the quality management goal by building the quality management system.

Project Scope

The *scope section* of a project plan defines the project's boundaries. It specifies what is included and what is excluded, such as activities or outcomes outside the project's objectives or constraints. The scope section also establishes a shared understanding of what the project will deliver. By defining the scope early in the planning process, the team can set realistic expectations, avoid scope creep, and improve the project's chances of success.

I previously worked with a team that specified in their project scope that they would only use e-learning course materials from one business line as the basis of their research for building a quality management system. They considered the implementation a pilot program and planned to repeat the process for other business lines and delivery modalities soon after, which would flow much easier because of what they'd learn the first time. I often recommend this approach, but you should make plans for how and when usage of the system will extend beyond the pilot.

One strategy for setting expectations is to use a *scope statement*, which ensures that everyone involved in the project clearly understands its reach. Here are some example scope statements:

- The project's objective is to develop a new hiring process to improve the candidate experience and reduce time-to-hire. The project will include defining job requirements, creating job postings, sourcing candidates, conducting interviews, and onboarding new hires. The project will exclude any changes to our compensation or benefits policies.
- The project will streamline our invoice processing system to reduce errors and increase efficiency. It will include mapping our current process, identifying bottlenecks, designing new workflows, implementing automation tools, and training our staff. The project will exclude any changes to our billing or accounting systems.
- The project will establish a product development process to bring new products to market faster. It will include defining product requirements, conducting market research, creating prototypes, testing products, and launching new products. The project will exclude changes to our existing products or manufacturing processes.
- The project will create a project management process for our organization to improve collaboration and communication among project teams. It will include defining project requirements, selecting a project management tool, designing workflows, providing training, and monitoring progress. The project will exclude any changes to our project budget or timelines.
- The project will establish a new customer service process to improve response times and customer satisfaction. It will analyze customer needs, create service-level agreements, design workflows, select communication channels, and train our staff. The project will exclude any changes to our products or pricing strategies.

Project Deliverables

The *project deliverables section* of a project plan lists the tangible outputs that the project will produce. The amount, type, and complexity of deliverables depends on the goal and the scope of the project. Ultimately, the deliverable should be a documented and formalized quality management system.

In chapter 2, I discussed the five characteristics of a formalized quality management system. It provided insight into what should be delivered to support the system's life cycle. Some example deliverables based on the five characteristics are:

- **A QA document** provides guidelines that support the standard. (Quality management systems are equipped with guidelines to measure against so people know what is expected and how to comply with the mission.)
- **A QC document** provides policies and procedures that support designers and developers as they navigate production. (Quality management systems are informed by documented policies, processes, procedures, and terms that support consistent workflow and communication.)
- **A QR checklist** for reviewers and approvers supports consistency. (Quality management systems are sustained by an additional process to support workflow and communication.)
- **Onboarding materials** for new internal or external designers, developers, and reviewers can be updated as processes change. (Quality management systems are designed to be scalable and flexible enough for inevitable change and growth.)
- **Tools and templates** can support most processes. (Quality management systems are supported by tools and templates to control quality as people navigate the process.)

Project Timeline

The *project timeline section* of a project plan outlines the schedule for the project, including key milestones and deadlines. It should identify the critical path and any dependencies among tasks. Depending on the project's goals and scope, there are many ways to distribute the work. The most intuitive strategy is to divide the work by phase:

1. **Quality planning**—create the standard.
2. **QA**—create guidelines to support the standard.
3. **QC**—create policies and procedures to support the guidelines.
4. **QR**—create mechanisms for checking for accuracy and ensuring guidelines and their supporting policies and procedures were followed.

There is no set timeline for creating a quality management system. The project's duration often depends on the project's scope, resources, and commitment in the face of competing priorities. Generally, however, there are three considerations for creating and managing the project timeline:

- Quality management is continuous.
- Assume the project will be deprioritized.
- There will likely never be a perfect time to build.

Quality Management Is Continuous

The project to build the initial system won't end—it will lay dormant. Even after the first draft, the process lead and owner must ensure the system is effective. It's a living, breathing (and eating) mechanism, so building and refining it will be just as much a part of the team's work as the quality management system itself. Realistically, there needs to be some indication of how long a project manager will need to focus on the initial launch.

Table 5-1 offers a recommendation for how to map out the overall project and how long each step takes.

Table 5-1. Project Steps

Step	Duration	Description
Creation	3 months	Create the system and the four phases: quality planning (creating standards), QA, QC, and QR.
Pilot Program	6 months	Select a learning experience to use as a pilot program for the new system. Identify realistic criteria to evaluate the results of the pilot program.
Evaluation	1 month	Evaluate the pilot program's success against the established criteria.
Revision	6 months	Revise the system based on the evaluation's results.
Launch	1 month	Officially launch the first iteration of the quality management system.
Integration	1 year	During this period, the process leads focus on encouraging people to use the system to transition it from an interesting experiment into the new normal.
Adoption	Ongoing	Fully adopt the system, achieve stability, and perform ongoing, periodic scheduled revisions.

TIP

In preparation for integration, develop a system for tracking what needs to be revised and then use it throughout the integration process. The criteria can be based on what was used to track the pilot program's success. Feel free to modify the system to ease the transition, but resist making extreme changes during integration unless implementation can't continue without them. Frequent changes will confuse people and dissuade them from using the system.

It could take up to three years to build, test, and adopt the system, depending on factors like scope, team size, and the learning function's organization. The steps are cyclical until the system is stabilized. The idea of spending three years on this project may come as a shock, but I suggest you and your team view this journey as a long-term investment. The pilot and revision periods will take the most time. You'll engage in the system, test it, and gather data on its effectiveness. Depending on various factors—like how you'll conduct research while simultaneously juggling competing priorities—the research required could take considerable time. Of course, you can shorten the time you'll be engaged in this project by limiting the scope. You can also save time by shortening some or all of the suggested timeframes. However, the time you save reducing the amount of research may be eaten up later if you have to prop up an unstable system.

Assume the Project Will Be Deprioritized

The second contributor to the length of the project is whether the project remains a priority throughout its development cycle. Most people will begin this project enthusiastically, but the L&D function is a service, so client needs may take precedence over developing the quality management system. Ironically, developing a quality management system actually creates a mechanism to better serve clients, but process owners and leads may have to constantly remind the team of those benefits (which were covered in chapter 1) while respecting the time constraints placed on them by L&D leadership and the organization at large.

Ultimately, the process owners and leads need to rely on their collective knowledge of how the L&D team prioritizes work and plan for these delays before they happen. Factor them into the timeline. Truthfully, rushing the team along using a variety of tactics is a short-term solution to the project being deprioritized. Encourage the team to develop a quality-first mindset—something they will need during the project's creation and implementation.

There Will Likely Never Be a Perfect Time to Build

There will be bad times to take on this project, like in the middle of a multi-curricular project. And, there will be better times, like when there is a lull in projects or when you're starting a team from scratch. But there will likely never be a perfect time, so do not wait for one. Plan for a time to build and implement controls to mitigate the risks.

Roles and Responsibilities

The *roles and responsibilities section* of the project plan specifies who is responsible for each task and what effort is required. One person should avoid attempting to create what will ultimately be a collaborative process by themselves. Even for a department of one, insight from SMEs familiar with the design process can be helpful.

Key Project Roles

There are three key project roles: process owner, process lead, and project manager. While exploring the roles people could play during this project, focus on the responsibilities rather than the titles. Most L&D teams cannot staff each role with a dedicated person or team, so either divide the responsibilities in a way that makes the most sense or reduce responsibilities by scaling back the scope and working in phases.

Process Owner

Throughout your quality management system's development and implementation cycle, the process owner has the most important role. They are responsible for documenting a business process according to the organization's standards (they may delegate the actual documenting but are responsible for its accuracy). During system development, they provide guidance, resources, and support to the project team. Quality management research stresses that having leadership's attention and advocacy is a crucial factor in the success of a quality management system, so their focus and feedback is required while the system is being assembled.

A process owner's specific roles and responsibilities in the development project may vary depending on the organization, project type, and project scope. However, some of the responsibilities of a process owner include:

- **Process analysis and design.** They ensure the current quality processes are analyzed and evaluated and the new system will target any current inefficiencies and gaps that compromise quality. While they should work closely with the process lead and project manager, they may operate more in a supervisory capacity.
- **Implementation.** They play an active role in implementing the process because they will ultimately own it. It is up to the process owner to ensure that the new process is implemented according to the project plan.

The process owner must be the person who leads the L&D function, whatever that looks like in your organization. There are situations in which this may not seem possible. For example, in many environments, an L&D professional is a department of one who reports to a person with no background (and, often, no interest) in learning and development. Alternatively, the L&D function may be decentralized. In that case, one or two L&D professionals may report to a manager in an entirely different department. As potentially undesirable as this sounds, the L&D function's leader still owns the process, just like they own every other process in learning and development. However, how they define that role will be based on the type of support the system needs. For example, the process owner's primary role could be advocacy from stakeholders, which may only require minimum involvement before, during, and after the project.

I have witnessed situations in which the function lead (whether they had an L&D background or not) did not want to take on the process owner role. What has worked for me is explaining that they already own all the functions in learning and development and quality management is no different. This is not a pet project that they can pay attention to when it suits them. I've explained that the sustainability of the system while dependent on their support. While I was not able to get these leaders to scream, "I am the process owner," from a mountain top, once I communicated that the system would not survive without an owner with enough power to make decisions about its direction and fate, they usually agreed.

Process Lead

The process lead will lead the quality management system throughout its life-time. During development, they work with the process owner to create and document guidelines to discuss with the other team members. They support the project manager with logistics, project tracking, and communication with the L&D stakeholders.

The process lead's responsibilities during system development include the following:

- **Project initiation and planning.** Collaborate with the project manager to initiate and plan the development of the quality management process. Create a project plan that outlines timelines, resource allocation, and key milestones. Ensure alignment with organizational objectives for quality improvement.
- **Stakeholder engagement.** Engage with key stakeholders, both internal and external, to gather input and requirements. Effective stakeholder communication and collaboration are essential for building a process that meets organizational and customer needs.
- **Regulatory compliance analysis.** Locate and analyze relevant industry standards and regulatory requirements pertaining to the quality of L&D products. Identify the specific criteria that the industry recognizes as best practices and ensure that the system aligns with them, if possible.

- **Process design and mapping.** Lead the design phase by defining the quality management process. Create detailed process maps, flowcharts, and documentation that outline how quality will be monitored, controlled, and improved. Design efficient workflows that minimize bottlenecks and redundancies.
- **Documentation development.** Lead the development of documentation for the system, including standard operating procedures (SOPs) and work instructions. Ensure that documentation is clear, accessible, and aligned with best practices.
- **Technology integration.** Oversee the integration of technology solutions (such as quality management software) that can enhance the efficiency and effectiveness of the quality management process, if applicable. Collaborate with IT teams to ensure seamless integration.
- **Training and awareness.** Develop training programs and materials to educate employees and stakeholders about the new quality management process. Conduct training sessions to ensure that individuals understand their roles and responsibilities within the process.
- **Change management.** Implement a change management strategy to facilitate the adoption of the new system. Communicate changes effectively to employees and stakeholders, addressing concerns and managing resistance.
- **Documentation maintenance.** Continuously update and maintain process documentation to reflect changes, improvements, and evolving best practices. Keep the documentation aligned with the actual process to ensure accuracy.
- **Reporting and communication.** Establish reporting mechanisms to communicate quality-related data and progress to relevant stakeholders. Regularly communicate quality performance and improvements to the team to maintain transparency.

Many teams may forego assigning the process lead role due to a lack of resources or other reasons. Remember, what gets watched, gets done. If no one is monitoring or watching the system on a continuous basis, it is at risk of fading away.

Here are a few tips for making the process lead role a reality:

- Integrate the responsibilities into a few people's existing roles. While initially a heavy lift, the weight will diminish over time.

- Hire a contractor to serve in the role for a predetermined amount of time to help you better understand what the role entails, and then pass it on to an internal resource as part of their role.
- Have administrative staff serve in the role. Ideally, the person in this role understands design and development so they can support the team as they navigate the system. However, being a designer or developer is not mandatory to be a process lead if that person knows who to ask for insight and advice when needed. If someone in another role learns the process, they can brainstorm with designers and developers to help resolve team challenges.

Project Manager

The project manager oversees the project, including planning, execution, monitoring, and control. They ensure the project is completed within the allocated budget, timeline, and scope. The project manager makes sure the objectives are achieved within the project's requirements. They also work closely with the process lead and process owner through the creation of the quality management system.

The key responsibilities of the project manager are:

- **Project planning.** Create a project plan that outlines the project's objective, which is to create a sustainable quality management system. The plan also describes the scope, timeline, and budget for building the process.
- **Resource management.** Manage the team, assign tasks, and ensure each team member has the necessary resources to accomplish their goals. The project manager may also lead the effort in determining who would be good candidates to join the team. The criteria vary, but including people who will play a role in or be affected by the new quality management system is necessary.
- **Risk management.** Identify potential risks and develop mitigation strategies. As the team builds the project, looking for risks will be an ongoing process. Other than the challenge of building a complex, collaborative system, the most significant risk is often maintaining momentum. (We'll look closer at risk management later in this chapter.)

- **Communication.** Communicate with stakeholders, including the project sponsor and team members, to inform them of project progress and any issues. Maintaining communication is essential for a project to be successful, but doing so also keeps it top of mind. (We'll take a closer look at communication later in the chapter.)
- **Budget management.** Manage the project budget and ensure that costs are kept within the approved limit. While building a quality management process isn't typically a budget-intensive project, new tools may be needed to manage the process. In addition, some teams elect to hire consultants to help them build it. (More on that later in the chapter.)
- **Project integrity.** Ensure the project meets the quality standards set by the organization. Unsurprisingly, the quality management process has its own standards to adhere to. For example, standards could include ensuring the process supports the quality mission, following the agreed-upon project plan, and progressing consistently toward the project's goals.

TIP

The process owner, process lead, and project manager roles are intended to be held by three different people. However, that is not always possible or desirable. For various reason (such as being an independent contractor, an internal team of one, or part of a small team with just a few people), there might not be anyone to take on these roles. One person can do it, but ensure the scope of the project, and ultimately the system itself, reflects that. In other cases, there may be people to take on the roles, but the structure of the team or the individual workloads can't easily accommodate them.

Focusing on responsibilities rather than roles may help you divide the work among several people. For example, two people could co-manage the project, or there could be a different process lead assigned to each business line or delivery modality (such as e-learning and instructor led). However, the process owner always resides with L&D leadership.

Other Roles

Besides the process owner, process lead, and project manager, there are roles for others as well. Some roles will also overlap. For example, the L&D manager may take on the project sponsor and the process owner roles. The stakeholders and SMEs may be the same people. The point of this section is to understand the responsibilities of each role so they can be distributed accordingly.

- **The project sponsor** is a key stakeholder in any project. They are responsible for providing the necessary resources, funding, and support to ensure the project's success. They act as the primary advocate for the project, promoting it to other stakeholders and ensuring the project aligns with the organization's goals and objectives. The sponsor will likely be an L&D or HR leader.

- **Stakeholders** are anyone with an interest in the project's success. The project stakeholders' role is to provide input, support, and feedback. Stakeholders can be internal or external to the organization and have various interests in the project. They may include customers, employees, suppliers, or other organization members. Stakeholders should be informed of the project's progress, and their input should be solicited throughout the process. The number of stakeholders for this project will depend on how the learning function is organized. For example, centralized teams may have fewer stakeholders than decentralized teams, who often have L&D leadership for every business line and need more voices to be heard. Of course, this assumes that the scope of the quality management system will include all teams, which isn't always the case.

- **SMEs** provide specialized knowledge and expertise in a particular area, which helps the project team make informed decisions. They guide and advise the project team on matters related to their area of expertise. They can be internal or external to the organization and are usually engaged as needed. This project will include internal practitioners or external consultants who design and develop training, business partners who work with the business line's leadership on behalf of learning and development, and content SMEs who may act as reviewers.

- **Team members** are responsible for executing the project tasks assigned to them by the project manager. They work collaboratively to complete project deliverables on time, within budget, and to the required quality.

They may be responsible for gathering data, conducting analysis, developing documentation, or testing the new process. In addition to the project and process leads, this group could include people on the L&D team who are not designers and developers, but whose insight or help can support the project, like LMS leads or administrative staff.

Finally, there's an optional business analyst role. This role is optional because it's a luxury to have a person dedicated to this work. The business analyst plays a crucial role in projects by serving as a liaison between the project team and the business stakeholders, helping to identify the business needs and project requirements. Their primary role is identifying, analyzing, and documenting business requirements and translating them into functional specifications that the project team can use to design and develop a solution. The project manager or process owner may take on this role in addition to their other work. The following is the typical configuration:

- The L&D manager serves as the process owner. Sometimes they are also the process lead, but this responsibility often shifts to a senior team member once they better understand the role's scope and workload.
- A senior learning designer is the project manager and the process lead. Other senior team members can fill this role too, like senior training consultants or relationship managers. However, if there is a project manager on the team, they usually take on that role.
- An external consultant can take on the project manager role for the project's duration. They can also stay on past implementation to help the process lead fully develop the role.
- Most of the L&D team members serve in some official role, like SME or stakeholder, depending on their experience and bandwidth. You want everyone to have a voice so the system is not just something happening to them.

Personnel Tools

Several resource management tools are available to help teams navigate projects with multiple people. A popular tool is a RACI chart or matrix—which is used to define and communicate roles and responsibilities for a project or process. The acronym RACI stands for responsible, accountable, consulted, and informed. The chart is typically a grid that lists tasks or deliverables along the top and roles along the side. Each cell in the grid indicates the level of responsibility for that task or deliverable for each role. Table 5-2 offers an example.

Table 5-2. Quality Management Project RACI Chart

Task or Activity	Responsible	Accountable	Consulted	Informed
Leading the project	Project manager	Project manager and process lead	Process owner	Stakeholders and project sponsors
Conducting research	Process lead, SME, and team members	Process owner and process lead	SMEs and team members	Stakeholders
Creating process flow diagrams	Process lead, SMEs, and team members	Process owner and process lead	SMEs and team members	N/A
Writing process documentation	Process lead, SMEs, and team members	Process owner and process lead	SMEs and team members	N/A
Reviewing and revising process documentation	Process lead, SMEs, and team members	Process owner and process lead	SMEs and team members	Stakeholders and project sponsors
Obtaining approval for process	Process lead and process owner	Process owner and senior management	Stakeholders	Stakeholders and project sponsors
Training team members on the new process	Process lead	Process owner and process lead	SMEs and team members	Stakeholders

At McCarthan Enterprises, Asia created a RACI chart for her project team, which you can find in her completed Getting Started worksheet in the appendix.

Risk Management

When I discuss the possibility of building a quality management system with anyone, the risks immediately come to mind. In my experience, taking time to improve a process requires taking time away from engaging in that process (which is typically the income generator)—and that can be a risky move. What if you invest a lot of time and resources into this project but can't complete the development process? What if you do complete it but don't reap the benefits you had hoped for? What if you don't get the promised support and you spend most of your time fighting to complete and maintain a system that no one values?

Effective risk management serves the following three critical purposes:

- Enhancing the project's ability to identify and assess potential threats or uncertainties that could jeopardize its success, allowing for timely mitigation strategies
- Supporting informed decision making by providing stakeholders with a clear understanding of the risks, ensuring resource allocation aligns with priorities
- Fostering stakeholder confidence and project transparency, thus promoting collaboration and reducing the likelihood of costly disruptions

TIP

Before I explore the extrinsic risks to success, it may be worthwhile to consider the intrinsic risks you'll personally face before even getting started.

When confronted with a challenge, we often ponder whether we can successfully complete it. This hesitation is rooted in psychological barriers because the intimidating nature of the task can trigger self-doubt and anxiety. We naturally assess our self-efficacy—gauging our belief in our capacity to succeed—before committing to a strategy. Additionally, a pragmatic evaluation of available resources (such as time, knowledge, skills, and tools) plays a pivotal role in the decision-making process.

Addressing these intrinsic risks to getting started requires a multifaceted approach. Begin by recognizing and managing psychological barriers, acknowledging that initial self-doubt is common. Cultivate a positive (and quality first) mindset through mindful self-awareness, positive self-talk, and visualization techniques like imagining what the workflow will look and feel like with a more efficient system. Enhance self-efficacy by doing adequate research, setting achievable milestones, and seeking guidance when needed (or just have someone available to talk to). Simultaneously, address resource evaluation by proactively assessing what will be needed and communicating what those needs will be (no one likes surprises). Finally, ask leadership for assistance with managing time and prioritizing tasks effectively.

The *risk management section* of a project plan identifies potential risks and outlines strategies for mitigating them. It addresses risks related to technology, people, processes, time, and other factors that could affect the project. The risk management documentation should be updated as needed throughout the project life cycle. The project's leadership and other relevant stakeholders should review and approve it. Ultimately, it should guide the project team's risk management activities.

The risk management section should be tailored to the specific project and its environment but will typically include the following elements:

- **Risk identification.** Identify and analyze potential external and internal risks that could influence the project. Risks can come from various sources, such as the project's scope, schedule, budget, resources, or environment.
- **Risk assessment.** Once all the potential risks have been identified, they need to be assessed in terms of their likelihood and impact, which helps the project team prioritize them and focus on the most probable and significant risks.
- **Risk mitigation.** Take steps to reduce the likelihood or impact of a risk. This can be done through various methods, such as changing the project scope, schedule, or budget; acquiring additional resources; or developing contingency plans. Mitigating risk may also involve transferring the risk to another party, reducing the likelihood or impact of the risk, or accepting that risk is unavoidable.
- **Risk monitoring and control.** The project team must regularly monitor identified risks and implement strategies to control them. This includes tracking progress and making adjustments as necessary, updating the risk register, re-evaluating risks, or implementing new mitigation strategies.

Returning to the McCarthan Enterprises case study, Asia and her team met with leadership to discuss risks to the project. They identified three significant risks: having time to complete the project, building a consensus on what the standards should be, and having reviewers beyond the L&D team participate in building and implementing the process. The team held several assessment and mitigation discussions around these identified risks to the project (Table 5-3). Asia believed that tracking risks would primarily be her responsibility as the learning function manager. However, the process lead and project manager were responsible for communicating when mitigation strategies should be implemented.

Table 5-3. McCarthan's Risk Management Plan

Risks	Assessment	Mitigation
Having time to complete the project	The likelihood of this happening is medium because, so far, leadership has demonstrated support for the project. However, if a more important issue arises, the risk increases.	• Develop criteria for determining whether a project should take focus over building a quality management system. This will reduce the likelihood of assuming that every new project should take focus. • The L&D team should discuss quality during team meetings, one-on-one meetings, and performance reviews. This will get the team used to having these discussions.
Building a consensus on what the standards should be	The likelihood of this happening is unknown because a discussion regarding quality has never been broached. However, because quality management depends on standards, mitigation strategies will have to be implemented if consensus cannot be reached.	• Develop a democratic data collection method so everyone's voices are heard, and communicate how everyone's input will be used. • Identify and communicate who will make the final decision on the scope and function of the process. • Process owners and leads should ensure and communicate that final decisions are grounded in science rather than opinion. • Be transparent while building the process.
Having reviewers beyond the L&D team participate in building and implementing the process	The likelihood of this happening depends on the support of the other teams' leadership. Their support is needed while building the system, but it will be more valuable during the pilot and adoption. Ideally, they can be persuaded after seeing the completed, successful process.	• Communicate the importance of this project to leadership early and often. • Ensure that the efforts asked of others are proportionate to the benefit they will receive. Put the focus on those parts of the organization that use training the most rather than expecting everyone to participate equally. • Keep the possibility of encountering resistance in mind while building the process and ensure that what's created is as streamlined and efficient as possible.

Budget

The *budget section* describes all the direct and indirect costs associated with a project. It should be prepared by the project manager and approved by the process lead, process owner, and project sponsor. It's a living document that is updated as needed throughout the project's life cycle.

Some items that are typically included in a project's budget section are:

- **Direct costs** are directly related to the project, such as materials, equipment, labor, and travel. Potential direct costs could include hiring or contracting an additional resource to consult on or guide the project in some capacity. Purchasing or subscribing to the tools needed to manage the project may also be necessary.
- **Indirect costs** are not directly related to the project but are necessary to complete the project, like overhead, administrative costs, and marketing costs.
- **Contingency funds** are set aside to cover unexpected costs, including changes in scope, schedule, or budget.
- **Budget allocation** is an outline of how the budget will be allocated across different project activities. The budget section should also include a contingency plan for unexpected expenses.
- **Total budget** is the sum of all direct, indirect, and contingency costs.
- **Reporting** is a plan that outlines how financial information will be communicated to stakeholders. This can include regular budget reports and updates to any significant budget changes.

At McCarthan Enterprises, the team was staffing all roles with internal employees so any costs incurred may be opportunity costs (the loss of potential gain from other alternatives when one alternative is chosen) because they chose to focus on building the system while foregoing other projects. The project manager used project management tools already available to them.

Communication Plan

The *communication plan section* describes the strategies and methods used for communicating with stakeholders and team members throughout the project life cycle. It should be prepared by the project manager, approved by the process lead and owner, and updated throughout the project life cycle.

At a minimum, a communication plan should contain these components:

- **Communication goals.** Defines the objectives of the communication plan, such as what messages need to be communicated and to whom. For McCarthan Enterprises, communication was the primary mitigation strategy to address the risk of stakeholders and other parties believing that the work to build and maintain a quality management system would not be worth the little value it would add to the organization—an idea based on the pervasive belief that the system would not be sustainable. Consequently, the communication goal was to consistently share the positive progress of the project, the helpful information learned along the way, and the benefits to the organization that a sustainable system provides.

- **Communication channels.** Describes the communication channels the team will use throughout the project, such as email, phone, video conferencing, or face-to-face meetings. For McCarthan Enterprises, email was the primary communication. However, the team also planned to lead online information sessions and post updates on the intranet, including the agenda for company-wide meetings.

- **Communication frequency or schedule.** Describes how often and when the team will receive communication. At McCarthan Enterprises, Asia understood the importance of balancing frequent communication with overcommunicating, but she didn't want to simply wait until the team had something new to report. They decided to develop a schedule for distributing information regarding the project and quality management in general.

- **Communication content.** Explains the content of the messages that will be communicated to stakeholders, such as project updates, status reports, or change requests. Refer to the project's RACI chart for who gets what. Asia's team at McCarthan Enterprises decided to to communicate other information about quality management along with updates about the project. Formalized quality management from a training perspective was a new concept for them, so some education on the topic and how it would affect their work lives helped with change management efforts.

CHAPTER 6
Assuring Quality

IN THIS CHAPTER:
- Scoping the standard
- Identifying, creating, and writing guidelines to support the standard
- Maintaining and revising the standard

Nearly every training department I've worked in decided at some point to create a mission. We'd coordinate an offsite meeting equipped with muffins and coffee and try to come to a consensus about the purpose of our organization's training function. At every company, the missions had two things in common. First, they were all more aspirational than practical and sounded something like this: "Our mission is to empower every member of our organization with the knowledge, skills, and resources they need to excel in their roles and drive the company's success. We are committed to fostering a culture of continuous learning, innovation, and professional growth, ensuring that our team members reach their full potential." Second, after that meeting, we never heard about the mission again.

What was missing was that we never figured out how to *operationalize the mission*—or turn abstract concepts into measurable elements, making it easier to study, manage, or achieve them. In other words, we never transformed those missions into action. Your quality management mission could suffer the same fate because a mission is only a statement if there is no standard that, when met, ensures it becomes a reality. It may be helpful to see a quality management system as a road map with a starting point and a destination and various routes to travel between them. Each route is paved with guidelines. One route may be recognized as the most efficient, but others, while circuitous, still ensure arrival.

This chapter maps out the journey to identifying or creating the standard and its supporting guidelines. Developing and implementing the standard is quality assurance, which consists of guidelines designed to provide confidence in the quality of products or services.

What Is a Standard?

While the term can be used in different ways, for our purposes, a *standard* is a set of guidelines, specifications, or criteria intended to ensure consistency, quality, safety, and, ultimately, performance. It's the overall body of knowledge that governs the quality management system. You may have heard of or complied with standards in learning and development or other industries.

In addition to providing a framework for achieving desired outcomes and promoting efficiency, a standard facilitates communication and collaboration. It provides a common language and framework for businesses, organizations, and individuals to understand and communicate expectations, requirements, and best practices. It gets everyone on the same page about how learning experiences should be built and what to expect once they are.

Here's a list of standards you may have encountered while in the corporate or nonprofit L&D industry:

- **WCAG (Web Content Accessibility Guidelines).** This web accessibility standard was created by the World Wide Web Consortium (W3C), which develops guidelines related to the web and internet technologies.
- **ANSI/IACET Standard for Continuing Education and Training.** Developed by the American National Standards Institute (ANSI) in partnership with the International Association for Continuing Education and Training (IACET), this standard sets the criteria and guidelines for developing, delivering, and evaluating high-quality continuing education and training programs.
- **Quality Matters (QM).** This standard developed by Quality Matters (a nonprofit organization dedicated to promoting QA in online education) is a set of guidelines and best practices for designing and delivering high-quality online courses. It provides a framework for course design, development, and review.
- **ISO 30422 Human Resource Management — Learning and Development.** This standard from the International Organization for

Standardization guides the learning and development organization in the workplace.

- **ISO TS 30437 Human Resource Management — Learning and Development Metrics.** This specification guides measuring the effectiveness of L&D programs. It is based on the measurement framework identified in ISO 30422 Human Resource Management — Learning and Development, and it includes efficiency, effectiveness, and outcome metrics.

To meet a standard, you must follow the guidelines that support it. So, for each individual standard, an experience needs to meet all the standard's guidelines to be compliant. There's no rule that you must adopt an all-or-nothing approach, although that is usually the goal. There may be reasons why a course doesn't fully meet the standard, like a sudden reduction in development time or resources. You can decide how compliant a course should be before it's eligible for release. The point is to acknowledge how and why the learning experience doesn't meet all the guidelines. Then, you can focus on developing strategies for working around actual or perceived barriers. Eventually, the team may have a playbook of what to do when full compliance is threatened.

NOTE

A guideline is not the same as a rule. A *guideline* is a reference point for comparison or evaluation and, consequently, implies flexibility for meeting it. A *rule*, on the other hand, is a specific directive or instruction that must be followed or obeyed. Rules are enforceable and carry consequences for noncompliance. Before beginning the process, be clear on which one your organization is creating and communicate it to stakeholders early and often.

It's essential to specify the consequences for noncompliance, if any. In my experience, people want to know how the system will affect them. They are often curious about what will happen to them if they cannot comply. However, they also know that policies without consequences for noncompliance have a low survival rate.

Scoping Your Standard

"We want standards, but we always get stuck on what we want standards for."
—Learning and development consultancy owner

There is no uniform model for what L&D looks like and how it operates across industries. Instead, the L&D department's design, function, and purpose varies across, and often within, organizations. If there is a formally recognized L&D function in an organization, it may range from one person to an international behemoth operating within a vast centralized hierarchy or a network of decentralized departments with complex reporting relationships. Some teams have a strict division of labor among design, delivery, and operations, whereas, in others, each practitioner is responsible for all tasks associated with their assigned projects. In addition, the learners served by the L&D function vary from all employees to specific departments to individual teams within those departments. Some teams serve parties outside the organization, like customers and vendors. Other teams only serve external clients and leave internal employee training to management. And L&D consultancies have their own challenges juggling different standards for their teams and for their clients.

As a result, there is no uniform standard that you can adopt for your quality management system. It must reflect the particulars of your organization. Unearthing the information to form your standard often leads to questions answered with more questions. A standard for what? And for whom? The answers to these questions will emerge from identifying the structure of your team's functional processes and deciding which ones fall within your prospective quality management system's scope.

Identifying Functional Processes

Scope defines the standard's boundaries by describing what will and will not be included. Your standard's scope will largely depend on the outcomes you want to achieve or, in other words, the mission of your quality management system. Many issues—like resources, timing, interest, and capability—will influence your choices.

Begin by completing a discovery exercise that includes mapping out how the L&D function currently works. Include the following information:

- The name of the function.
- The organizational model of the training group and how it supports the business.
  - *A centralized training organization* constitutes one training function residing in a single group, meaning all resources and processes are managed within one organization.
  - *The decentralized model* consists of multiple training teams, each managed and funded by a different business line.
  - *The federated model* combines the two models by centralizing some processes and platforms and decentralizing others. For example, design and development might be managed by different teams within the business lines, but all teams use the same LMS.
- The roles (not people) responsible for the function (such as team leads and senior learning designers).
- A process map that shows the connections among groups and when and how they occur.

In addition to gaining further clarity into how the department currently operates, you may identify (or confirm) inefficiencies before you begin the project. You'll also potentially gather data supporting the need for a quality management system. When I worked at an international organization, we discovered (after someone got curious enough to take inventory) that more than 100 different installations of various learning management systems were being used. It was a large organization, so perhaps this was necessary; however, with such poor communication among the training organizations, there couldn't have been much knowledge sharing or consistency in our strategies. This had to influence quality—and not for the better.

Returning to the case study, McCarthan Enterprises used a centralized model, although some learning designers and facilitators focused on corporate, while others focused on retail. I discussed their team hierarchy in more detail in chapter 3, and you can find their org chart in Figure 3-2.

Once you've completed the discovery exercise, work with your team to group and categorize functions. How your team decides to do this is up to you, but some frameworks may help. As part of Training Industry's Certified Professional in Training Management program, participants explore a diagram called the Training Process Framework, which codifies the following functional processes L&D teams usually manage (and this is consistent with my experience):

- **Administration processes** are associated with managing the logistics and day-to-day operations of a training function. For Asia's team, this process included the L&D manager, administrative assistant, L&D business partners, and training coordinators.
- **Content processes** are related to creating, curating, and managing content. These might include courses, workshops, seminars, webinars, or programs. For Asia's team, this process included the learning experience and project management teams. The project managers could be included in the administration team, but at McCarthan, they were more engaged in navigating content management than administrative tasks. Also, while the technology team did help procure and often support e-learning development tools, the learning experience team focused on using them.
- **Delivery processes** are related to the transfer of information, including instruction and delivery of content. For Asia's team, this process included the learning facilitation team.
- **Technology processes** include systems used to create, manage, and deliver training. For Asia's team, this included the learning technology team.

Not all L&D departments align with the framework, but most include these functions in some capacity. View them as functions and not necessarily individual departments. The content and delivery functions are often combined, and there may not be a separate technology function, leaving the administration function to handle registrations and the content function to support their own technology.

To better understand what function Asia should include in the scope of the quality management function, let's revisit her team's mission: "To ensure targeted training materials created and managed by the L&D team support the organization's performance through learning and development with the collaborative participation of McCarthan Enterprises' leadership."

Based on the mission, focusing on the content functional process group is the most obvious choice, but doing so has far-reaching implications. What if the content meets standards, but the facilitator's delivery style is not engaging? What if the LMS user experience discourages people from enrolling in courses?

Having a solid, well-researched mission comes in handy because decisions like this will be easier to make. The mission refers to "targeted training materials created and managed by the L&D team," so content should be the focus; however, there are other considerations. Let's look at them now.

Functional Lenses

A learning experience consists of different components, and each one should be evaluated with its own criteria. Consider an e-learning course on communication skills, for example. Within that experience, there are several components, including images, words, and navigation. The images, for example, may be aesthetically pleasing, but the navigation is confusing. So, the course needs guidelines for each of those components to meet a standard.

Because the McCarthan Enterprises case study focuses on training materials, which fall within the content function, let's explore the following possible lenses through which Asia's team can view their content:

- **Effectiveness.** Their search for effectiveness requires looking at a course through a *learning design lens*.

- **Visual appeal and communication.** Determining how the imagery and other graphics in the course enhance the learning experience and contribute to effectiveness requires a *visual design lens.*
- **Interface and navigation strategies.** The learner's journey through a course from beginning to end can be evaluated through an *interface design lens.*
- **Written and verbal communication.** Ensuring courses are written consistently through word choices and voice requires a *communications strategy lens.*

These are possible lenses and you can decide how you want to view the work produced by each function. You can also name the lenses whatever you want. Categorizing products in this way makes it easier to apply guidelines to groups of assets. For example, you may want to avoid having a set of guidelines for how to write a participant guide and then another set for leader guides. One set of communication strategy guidelines may cover all written communication produced for learning purposes.

TIP

Another method to classify outcomes are the Talent Development Reporting principles (TDRp):
- Efficiency measures provide insight into the quantity of delivered training programs and their use, cost, and reach within the organization.
- Effectiveness measures provide insight into the quality of the programs using models such as Kirkpatrick's four levels of evaluation or the Phillips ROI (return on investment) Methodology.
- Outcome measures demonstrate the impact of learning on business or HR goals.

More on measuring quality using these classifications can be found in David L. Vance and Peggy Parskey's 2020 book *Measurement Demystified: Creating Your L&D Measurement, Analytics, and Reporting Strategy.*

Let's explore a high-level overview of the suggested lenses for content guidelines.

Learning Design Lens

For simplicity's sake, *learning design* is a stand-in term for the many methodologies used to create learning experiences. For example, some organizations describe what they do as *instructional design*, while others say *learning experience design*. Some practice *learning architecture*. In the McCarthan Enterprises case study, Asia's predecessor committed to using *learning design*, which consists of planning, designing, and developing effective and engaging experiences that support learning, ultimately leading to improved performance outcomes. The desire for a learning design standard often drives the need for a quality management system. While many factors contribute to a learning experience's quality and outcomes, the L&D function has the most control over the design and delivery of content, so that's often where teams choose to start.

When identifying guidelines for effective learning design, there's often a temptation to create a list that eradicates pet peeves or enforces strategies that are based more on preference than theory. This results in guidelines connected only because they refer to learning design and appear on the same list.

While you may list individual guidelines, it may be a better strategy to derive them from existing standards or a specific evidenced-based approach or methodology. For example, to source guidelines, you can:

- **Adopt an existing standard.** While there is no one universal standard followed by the entire L&D industry, a few organizations have developed applicable guidelines. For example, as I mentioned earlier in this chapter, IACET has a standard (the ANSI/IACET Standard for Continuing Education and Training). Quality Matters also has a standard specifically for online courses. There's also TDRp, which provides guidelines for measuring and reporting the effectiveness and impact of L&D initiatives within an organization, as well as ISO's standards for learning and development.

- **Amend an existing standard.** Take an existing standard and modify it to suit your organization's needs. You may also combine several standards into one.

- **Follow the principles of a design approach.** Assemble best practices for instructional design or learning experience design and use them to create guidelines to build an applicable standard.

- **Adopt existing learning theories, frameworks, or principles.**
  Take one or more of the foundational theories for learning
  (behaviorism, cognitivism, and constructivism) and find or create
  guidelines based on them to design a standard. You may also use
  popular frameworks like Gagne's Nine Events of Instruction or M.
  David Merrill's First Principles of Instruction to develop a standard
  that guides learning design.

I've often encouraged clients to use the last approach because the terminology and methodologies are usually easier to apply. My go-to is Merrill's First Principles of Instruction because they prioritize problem solving, activating prior knowledge, authentic application, clear guidance, reflection, practice, and learner engagement.

NOTE

Remember, having a standard does not mean designing first and then determining whether the output meets the mark, so create a standard that supports the organization's goals, and then design to meet the standard. QA and QC occur during the design process, not after.

Unfortunately, there is no way to build a standard that will guarantee learning and improved performance. There are too many factors outside the standard's scope that influence these outcomes. The guidelines that make up the standard should be characteristics that, when present in a learning experience, support the type of outcomes you are seeking.

This perspective allows you and your team to let your guidelines evolve. While a standard is not intended to stifle experimentation and creativity, you must remember learning design is more of a science than an art. The lack of standardization probably makes it seem like you can all have your own way of doing things, but perspectives change as you learn more.

Visual Design Lens

Visual design is not just about making content pretty. It's arranging and combining visual elements (such as colors, typography, images, and layout) to effectively communicate ideas, enhance aesthetics, and facilitate learner engagement and comprehension.

There is no universal visual design standard or specific guidelines for learning materials. The L&D industry recognizes the role of visual design in learning comprehension; however, there are varying opinions on what a learning designer should be able to create and how well they should be able to do it. After all, visual design is an entirely different skill set than learning design, and the lack of a standard makes it difficult to gain or evaluate competence.

There are visual design guidelines that can be applied to training documents, presentations, and online learning modules. While many sources exist for this information, one set of universally recognized principles is the Gestalt (German for "unified whole") principles, which describe how humans perceive and interpret visual information. A group of German psychologists developed these principles in the early 20th century, and they have since become fundamental visual design concepts. Any of them can be used as the basis for visual design guidelines. A key consideration is to make the connection between visual design and learning outcomes clear for those using the standard.

Here are some specific examples of how to apply four Gestalt principles to training materials:

- **Proximity.** Group related items together on a page or screen. For example, place text close to the images or diagrams it refers to. Chunk information into clear sections.
- **Similarity.** Use similar design elements to group together related items. For example, you could use the same font style and color for all headings in a training document.

- **Continuity.** Use lines and arrows to guide learners' eyes through your training materials. For example, you could use arrows to show learners the sequence of steps in a process.
- **Figure-ground.** Use contrast to make important information stand out. For example, use contrast, white space, and visual hierarchy to emphasize important text or images.

NOTE

There are several reasons why including visual design guidelines for inclusive and diverse imagery is a worthwhile strategy to ensure everyone can see themselves reflected in the content, including:

- **Representation matters.** Inclusive and diverse imagery ensures that learners from all backgrounds, ethnicities, genders, abilities, and cultures feel represented and included in the learning experience. By featuring a wide range of people in your e-learning content, you send a message that everyone's experiences and perspectives are valued, which can foster a sense of belonging, encourage engagement, and create a more inclusive learning environment.
- **Challenge stereotypes and biases.** Incorporating diverse imagery challenges stereotypes and biases by showcasing individuals from different backgrounds, which could help break down preconceived notions and promote a more accurate and nuanced understanding of different cultures, identities, and abilities. This promotes empathy, respect, and appreciation for diversity, which are vital skills in a globalized world.
- **Increase engagement and motivation.** When learners see themselves reflected in the course content, they may be more likely to feel connected and engaged. Inclusive imagery allows learners to identify with the material and relate it to their own experiences, making the learning process more relatable and meaningful. This can positively influence motivation, active participation, and better knowledge retention.

Visual design work can be delegated to visual design professionals who are experts in their fields, but that is a luxury for many teams. Consequently, learning designers should know how to apply the basics, but you'll have to determine what role these principles play in your standard.

Interface Design Lens

I had developed e-learning content for years before I heard about interface design. As part of my master's in education program, I took an introductory course in the human and computer interaction graduate program out of curiosity. We focused on building screens for software and websites. I didn't know then that I would soon be building interfaces myself when developing e-learning content. Because of what I learned in that course, I always saw the interface as an intimate relationship between the learner and the content. Designers aren't there to tell the learner how to navigate a course—only the interface can do that, and it's our job to ensure that it does.

Interface design means creating visually and functionally effective interfaces for digital products. Interface designers focus on graphical layouts, interactive elements, and overall user experience. Their goal is to design an intuitive, visually appealing, cohesive, and interactive experience between users and the interface that, in this context, facilitates better learning outcomes. Interface design is more applicable to organizations that develop e-learning content or other digital learning experiences.

NOTE

As I mentioned, interface design usually refers to digital experiences, but many teams focus primarily on print products. A close cousin of interface design is *document design*, which is the deliberate and strategic arrangement of visual and textual elements within a document to communicate information and facilitate understanding effectively. It includes the layout, formatting, typography, graphics, and overall aesthetics of a document, whether it's a printed page, a digital report, a presentation, or another type of written or visual communication. Effective document design aims to enhance readability, clarity, and the overall user experience, making it easier for readers to grasp the content, absorb vital messages, and navigate the information. You may want to add document design as an additional lens or expand the interface design lens to include document design guidelines.

Interface design is also its own discipline governed by its own body of knowledge and guidelines. As I mentioned in the visual design section, being a good learning designer should not require being a good interface designer. However, there is a recognized function in learning and development that does require interface design and visual design knowledge and skill: learning or e-learning development. Some organizations include development tasks in the learning designer role, while others have created a developer role separate from designers.

For some, being expected to master learning and interface design is a daunting task, and like with visual design, there's no standard, making it difficult to gain or evaluate competence. Interface design can also be delegated to external resources, while internal learning designers focus on learning outcomes. Ultimately, those who develop are responsible for meeting interface design guidelines.

In addition to principles borrowed from visual design, interface design is also related to the following disciplines:

- **Interaction design.** Designing interactive elements (such as buttons, dropdown menus, sliders, and forms), defining their behavior and ensuring intuitive and efficient user interactions. Considerations for feedback, responsiveness, and micro-interactions are also important.
- **Navigation design.** Designing intuitive and efficient ways for learners to move between different pages, sections, or screens within a course.
- **Usability.** Focusing on making the interface usable and accessible to diverse users. It considers clear and concise messaging, intuitive workflows, and proper contrast ratios.
- **Responsive design.** Adapting the interface to different screen sizes and devices, ensuring a consistent and optimized experience across desktop, mobile, and other platforms.

The laws of interface design are also good sources for guidelines, including:

- **Hick's Law.** The time it takes to make a decision increases with the number of choices available, so reduce complexity by providing clear and concise options.
- **Fitts's Law.** The time required to move to a target is influenced by its distance and size, so it's essential to make frequently used targets larger and place them closer to the starting point for efficient interaction.

- **Jakob's Law.** Users better adapt to interfaces that follow familiar design patterns, so reduce the learning curve by being consistent across courses and complying with established conventions.
- **Consistency Principle.** Maintain consistency in the interface elements, layout, terminology, and interaction patterns within a system to help users develop mental models that enable them to use their knowledge across different interface elements.
- **Simplicity Principle.** Keep interfaces simple without sacrificing functionality to help reduce cognitive load and improve the overall user experience.

TIP

Accessibility should be a primary consideration in creating print and digital L&D materials, so adding it to your standard is essential. In an L&D context, *accessibility* refers to the design and presentation of learning content in a way that ensures everyone can access, comprehend, and engage with the material effectively. It requires removing barriers and providing inclusive features that accommodate all visual, auditory, cognitive, and motor abilities. This contributes to ensuring equitable access and learning opportunities for all individuals.

Before adding accessibility guidelines, it may be helpful to decide on an overall strategy or policy regarding accessibility, which will help you avoid a piecemeal approach with no coherent plan. In the US, government agencies require compliance with Section 508 of the Rehabilitation Act of 1973. The law mandates that federal agencies make their electronic information accessible to individuals with disabilities. Other entities have no such requirements, which means they are free to use some, all, or none of the guidelines listed in the act. Your organization should consider what works best, but remember, accessibility helps everyone. Research accessibility and learning materials further to learn more about including guidelines in your standard.

You'll have to determine whether accessibility should be added as a separate review process or as part of multiple reviews. The latter is preferred because it conveys that accessibility is part of the overall design approach and not a last-minute consideration.

Communication Strategy Lens

When I moved to Chicago, Illinois, from Detroit, Michigan, I had dreams of writing or acting. I did neither. About 15 years later, I learned that a local university offered a master of arts degree in writing. While I was tempted to enroll in the program, I thought, for some reason, that a person should only have one master's degree. I already had one, and having two seemed eccentric. Soon after making that decision, however, I suddenly started meeting other people with multiple master's degrees. In the end, I decided that getting a writing degree would fulfill a promise I made myself when I moved to Chicago. And while I could have also just started writing, I was drawn to the program's requirement to explore different genres. So, I enrolled.

I'm not sure whether completing the program made me a better writer, but it did make me a better learning designer. Being able to view the world through the eyes of others is essential to writing stories, and I apply the same strategy when designing instruction. Writing is more than putting words on the page; it's word choice, tone, style, and (for nonfiction writing) a conversation between the reader and author. Although learning designers spend a lot of time writing, it's not a skill they inherently have.

Like with visual design and interface design, others assume that learning designers can write well despite the absence of a documented standard describing what that means. Professionals who communicate well are probably drawn to learning design, so it's less of a consideration. However, many enter the field through e-learning development or learning technology roles—which do not typically require learning design skills—and may be thrust into the designer role by their organization. So, despite not being drawn to learning design, it becomes their job, and they spend most of their time writing.

Determining whether someone is a good writer is an unhelpful exercise in subjectivity. However, determining whether writing meets a set of guidelines is more objective. Guidelines communicate to learning designers what's expected of them. While there is no universal standard for writing, luckily, there are time-tested guidelines for effective writing that can be applied to learning materials.

There are various writing style guides, including:

- *MLA Style Manual and Guide to Scholarly Publishing* for humanities and liberal arts disciplines

- *Publication Manual of the American Psychological Association* for the social sciences
- *The Chicago Manual of Style* for the publishing industry
- *The Associated Press Stylebook and Briefing on Media Law* for journalism

Other style guides for technical writing include:

- *IEEE (Institute of Electrical and Electronics Engineers) Reference Guide* for engineering, computer science, and related fields
- *Microsoft Writing Style Guide* for technical communication, specifically software and hardware documentation
- *The IBM Style Guide: Conventions for Writers and Editors* for documentation related to IBM products and services
- *Apple Style Guide* for Apple products and platform documentation
- *Google Developer Documentation Style Guide* for documentation related to Google platforms and application programming interfaces (APIs)

Most of these style guides are available to the public in part, either in print form or online. *The Microsoft Writing Style Guide* has been beneficial to me throughout my career; I've used it for both technical and professional development training. You can adopt, amend, and borrow from any style guide. Some organizations also use an in-house style guide, and if this is true for your organization, it may be more efficient (and often mandatory) for you to start there. Style guides are usually long, comprehensive documents, so you may want to focus on the guidelines that you'll use regularly for writing training material. For example, include punctuation and capitalization guidelines, but exclude information on formatting citations.

TIP

A critical factor in meeting a standard is possessing the knowledge and skills to complete the tasks that the guidelines require. For example, a learning designer cannot meet any standard regarding learning objectives if they were placed in that role without substantial training on how to write them. However, it's inadvisable to use a standard to teach skills. You can use it to identify skills gaps and support designers as they obtain new skills, but implementing a standard should not replace professional development training, nor should it ever be punitive.

Forming and Managing a Committee

Following and maintaining a standard is collaborative, so creating one should be too. In chapter 5, we covered many roles that should be filled for the quality management system development project, like the stakeholders, SMEs, and other team members. After filling those roles, the process owner, process lead, and project manager must work with the rest of the team to develop the process and build consensus. Essentially, you should form a committee that includes representatives from all relevant groups.

Best Practices for Forming a Committee

For some, forming a committee may be simple due to your organization's structure. The leads are already identified. You have a dedicated project manager. Perhaps a quality management system was the L&D manager's idea, so they are happy to be the process owner. For others, forming the committee may be more challenging. As I mentioned earlier, the most significant challenges are finding people and time. There are some best practices that can help you efficiently form a committee, including:

- **Define the committee's purpose and scope.** Document the specific goals, objectives, and expected outcomes.
- **Establish clear roles and responsibilities for committee members.** To ensure accountability and efficiency, delegate specific work, such as research, data collection, drafting, reviewing, note taking, and facilitating meetings.
- **Set a realistic project timeline.** Consider the complexity of tasks, the availability of resources, and the need for thorough discussions and reviews.
- **Provide adequate resources.** Ensure the committee can access the necessary resources, information, and people to fulfill its goal.
- **Foster collaboration and communication.** Encourage and support open and transparent communication within the committee. Create an environment where all members feel comfortable expressing their opinions, ideas, and concerns.

Best Practices for Managing the Committee

Once the committee is formed, it needs to be well managed to reach its goals. This includes leading organized and productive meetings and guiding members as they tackle their individual assignments. Here are a few best practices to adopt for managing the committee:

- **Establish communication channels**—like regular meetings, email updates, online collaboration tools, or project management software—to facilitate collaboration and information sharing among committee members.
- **Set and follow an agenda.** Share the agenda before all meetings to ensure members stay focused and productive. Stick to it during meetings, allocate sufficient time for discussions, and keep the meeting on track.
- **Foster collaboration and inclusion.** Create an inclusive and respectful environment where all ideas and perspectives are valued. Encourage members to share their expertise and contribute to the decision-making process.
- **Manage conflict and disagreements.** Be prepared to address conflicts promptly and objectively. Encourage open dialogue, active listening, and respectful communication.
- **Monitor progress and provide constructive feedback.** Acknowledge and celebrate milestones and achievements.
- **Facilitate and encourage decision making.** Ensure decisions are made based on consensus whenever possible. If consensus cannot be reached, consider alternative decision-making methods, such as voting or seeking external input. Communicate the rationale behind any decisions and make sure all members understand them.
- **Ensure buy-in and implementation.** Once the committee has developed the standard, gain buy-in and support from key stakeholders and decision makers.
- **Recognize and appreciate member contributions.** Publicly acknowledge their achievements and the value they bring to the committee's work.

Developing a Standard

Once the scope is identified and the committee is formed, develop the standard. I recommend following a four-step process, but it is not the only option. This process is not unique to quality management—it's simply a way to organize the work as you develop the guidelines that you'll use to create your standard:

1. Identifying guidelines
2. Writing guidelines
3. Verifying or testing guidelines
4. Finalizing the standard

Identifying Guidelines

For many, the issue isn't a lack of a standard; instead, it's the lack of a documented standard that's accepted by everyone and consistently applied to every product. In the previous section, I discussed sources you can use or refer to as inspiration for guidelines, but the best place to start is at home.

Identifying Existing Internal Guidelines

"We all have guidelines. They're just all in our heads. We know what's right when we see it."

—Senior instructional designer

I also have a personal guideline database that lives in my head based on decades of experience and education. By identifying existing internal guidelines, you can unearth all the information that's stored in people's minds and notes, and document it so the best practices can be used to inform guidelines that can enhance everyone else's work. Here are some suggestions for accessing existing data that you can use as a foundation for your guidelines:

- **Gather information from people whose roles fall within scope.** You can collect this information in surveys and interviews. During these initial discussions, you're not asking what guidelines they'd like to use or see implemented. Instead, ask for best practices they've tried and what's worked for them so you can accurately assess the current state.
- **Review existing materials.** Examine materials (like job aids) that have generated a positive result and identify what contributed to success.

- **Gather feedback from people who use the materials.** This group includes learners.
- **Ask internal communications or marketing professionals if they have documented standards.** You may already be painfully aware of the lack of or over abundance of documented standards. While learning materials are not marketing resources or other internal communications, many L&D departments must adhere to company-wide standards.

Identifying Existing External Guidelines

While the wealth of information you'll find inside the organization will add tremendous value to your internal body of knowledge, there are several reasons to also reference external guidelines, including:

- They are typically evidence based and time tested instead, rather than opinions or personal preferences.
- The standard should be bigger than the current team, going beyond what a specific group of people at a given point in time want. Instead, it should focus on what is best for the L&D function regardless of who joins the team.
- They can save you time. Learning about where you are currently as a team, determining where you want to be, and writing a standard based on that is challenging and time consuming. However, if you instead base the standard on existing guidelines, the primary challenge becomes meeting the standard.

Backing Your Standard

While the L&D team's education and experience matters, the standard and the guidelines that support it should be evidence based—meaning they rely on empirical evidence, studies, research, experiments, objective data, and credible sources. This approach minimizes bias, subjectivity, and unsupported assumptions, and ultimately leads to more reliable and effective outcomes.

Having an evidenced-based standard is another way for the L&D team to gain or maintain credibility. It's no secret that many outside the industry believe learning design is a fancy term for making pretty PowerPoints. A standard based on evidence puts the team in a stronger position to steer stakeholders away from any long-held or inaccurate beliefs.

For a guideline to be considered evidence based, data should prove that the guideline will contribute to a desired outcome when it's applied. So, when you look for existing internal guidelines, it's essential to distinguish opinions and anecdotal data from evidence. For example, if a designer says that "including knowledge checks throughout an e-learning module worked really well," that's not evidence. Using an evidence-based approach, a designer instead would say, "In the pilot version of the course, there were no knowledge checks—just the final quiz. The pilot test scores were low, and in their feedback, participants said that knowledge checks throughout the course may help them better prepare for the final quiz. So, we added them into the second pilot version, and the quiz scores improved by 50 percent." Of course, this example is not a valid study given the small number of times the pilot program was run and the inability to exclude other factors that may have contributed to the new score. Still, it provides more evidence than "it worked really well."

TIP

You may not have the data you need to support existing internal practices. But all is not lost! If the best practices you identify seem worth adding to the standard, research them to determine if they can be backed by any data from external sources. For example, using the pilot program scenario regarding frequent knowledge checks, research exists that recognizes the value of practice on learning outcomes.

Writing Guidelines

In this section, I want to return to Asia and her team at McCarthan Enterprises to discuss what they decided to use when writing their guidelines. There isn't one structure for guidelines, but most should include at least two components:

- **An identifier.** Begin each guideline with a unique identifier or code for easy reference and organization. For example, Asia decided to identify the learning design guidelines for her team's standards with the code LD followed by a number. If you include subguidelines, use decimal points, like LD 1.0 followed by LD 1.1, and LD 1.2.

- **The guideline text.** Describe the outcome of applying the guideline. Use specific and measurable language and start each one with an action verb. For example, one of the Asia's guidelines is "Write learning objectives that target a single behavior using the ABCD (audience, behavior, condition, degree) format, omitting elements when they're assumed or not applicable." This guideline tells the designer what is expected of them and tells reviewers what they should expect to see.

Clarifying Guidelines

While some guidelines may not need to be broken down further or explained, most will need additional clarification for learning designers and the reviewers. To make guidelines as clear as possible, enhance them by adding the following information:

- **Criteria** serve as indicators to determine whether specific requirements or expectations are met.
- **Qualifiers** provide additional context, clarification, or limitations. They help refine the guideline, ensuring that it is properly interpreted and applied in specific situations.
- **Conditions or limitations** clarify the circumstances under which a guideline applies. For example, guidelines may be applied differently based on the delivery modality or medium (such as font sizes and branding choices).
- **Time limits** define a specific timeframe within which a guideline should be met. This is useful for specifying turnaround times for deliverables, for example.
- **Exceptions or special cases** account for circumstances that may affect the guideline. This is particularly important when they need to accommodate diverse situations or be flexible enough to meet the business's needs.

> **NOTE**
>
> It's important to be specific when creating guidelines. However, don't rely on subjective adjectives to describe how the work should be accomplished because you will need to provide specifics when asked. For example, phrases like "modern imagery" or "engaging activities" must be defined for people to meet the guidelines.

McCarthan's Guidelines

Let's review two of Asia's guidelines. First, LD 2.0 states, "Write learning objectives that target a single behavior using the ABCD (audience, behavior, condition, degree) format, omitting elements when they're assumed or not applicable." Table 6-1 provides some background information to explain how the team constructed this guideline.

Table 6-1. Guideline LD 2.0

Component	Background
LD 2.0	LD is the identifier for learning design.
Write learning objectives. . .	Asia and Jabari, the learning design lead, frequently come across poorly written learning objectives, so they created a guideline for writing effective objectives to support the mission.
. . . that target a single behavior. . .	Jabari often sees compound learning objectives that target multiple behaviors simultaneously, and he wants to end that practice.
. . . using the ABCD (audience, behavior, condition, degree) format. . .	Jabari learned about the ABCD format in an instructional design course and thought it would be a useful way to standardize the learning objectives.
. . . omitting elements when they're assumed or not applicable.	While Asia appreciates standardization, she anticipates situations in which the audience is the same for every objective and doesn't need to be repeated, or the condition and degree aren't relevant. However, she supports including the ABCD format in the guideline because she would like to encourage the team to put more effort into identifying all four components. This part of the guideline is a qualifier because it is an additional condition or factor that modifies or adds specificity to the guideline.

NOTE

Notice that Asia's guideline includes no mention of the quality of the objective itself, whether it's the correct objective for this course, or whether the objective is present in the course. It strictly focuses on how the objective is written. The other criteria can be covered in another guideline or not included at all. Every aspect of a learning experience does not warrant a guideline.

One litmus test for creating a guideline is whether the action described can be tracked. For example, a guideline that requires judging the validity of a learning objective would require criteria for the designer to comply with the guideline and criteria for the reviewer to judge whether the guideline has been met. Don't let guideline development cloud your judgment regarding the competency of your team. Too many guidelines can feel like micromanagement, which is not required to have a quality management system. Remember, include guidelines only for what you want to control.

Another one of Asia's guidelines, VD 1.0, states, "Ensure text is readable by using legible, nondecorative fonts. For print and digital learning experiences, use a font size that will remain legible in different sizes and on different devices. For presentations, ensure the font is large enough to be read from the back of a large room." Table 6-2 breaks down the background information Asia's team used to arrive at the different components.

Table 6-2. Guideline VD 1.0

Component	Background
VD 1.0	VD is the identifier for visual design.
Ensure text is readable by using legible, nondecorative fonts.	Asia and the learning design lead have occasionally come across illegible decorative fonts. Because it's so rare, they debated writing this guideline but decided to include it for new hires and vendors. They also realize that some individuals may not be familiar with the term "decorative font" or be able to visually identify one.
For print and digital learning experiences, use a font that will remain legible in different sizes and on different devices.	The team debated whether font size should be coupled with font type. Both address text readability, so they decided to combine them to limit the number of guidelines. They initially listed a minimum font size but realized that optimal font size often depends on how it's being displayed. They know that reviewers won't be able to verify the font size by looking at it, which leaves the guideline open to interpretation, but they chose to take that risk for now.
For presentations, ensure the text is large enough to be read from the back of a large room.	Presentations with small fonts have been a problem that Asia and Jabari have wanted to address for a long time. They understand that as written, it's open to interpretation because developers and reviewers may not be able to discern whether the text can be viewed across a room. They are relying on people using their best judgement but are open to revisiting the guideline if necessary.

The guideline should say what should happen rather than what should not happen. Instead of writing, "Do not use clipart," write, "Use photographic images that reflect the work environment of the learners." However, a learning designer who adheres to the guideline may still fall short of expectations. In this case, they may select the types of photographs others deem inappropriate.

One concern about guidelines that learning designers often express is the loss of creative freedom in making design choices. Chapter 9 will address balancing creative freedom with the need for consistent guideline application.

Verifying or Testing Guidelines

A standard is an important document, and untested guidelines have no place in it. However, subjecting each guideline to a validity test is time consuming and often discourages many from moving forward. I've told my clients to verify the guidelines instead.

Verifying means ensuring or demonstrating something is true, accurate, or justified. In this context, verifying could mean locating the internal or external source of the best practice described in the guideline. It could also mean continuously tracking the guideline's viability after the standard is implemented to ensure that applying it consistently contributes to the intended outcome.

I find that generating guidelines from reliable course sources helps with the verification process. However, if you choose to test some or all of the guidelines, here is a general framework to follow:

1. **Establish clear objectives.** Define the purpose and goals of the testing process and specify the criteria for success.
2. **Develop test plans.** Create detailed plans describing how the tests should be carried out, including the methodologies, tools, and required resources. A test plan often includes test objectives, cases, data, and specific test conditions or scenarios.
3. **Design test cases.** Develop well-defined test cases that resemble the situations in which the guideline may need to be applied.

4. **Execute the test.** Execute the test cases according to the defined test plans. Record the results of each test, including any deviations or issues encountered during testing.
5. **Evaluate test results.** Analyze the results to determine whether the guideline meets expectations by comparing the actual results with the expected results from the test cases.
6. **Document findings.** Document the test results, including any identified issues and recommendations for improvement or remediation.
7. **Implement corrective measures.** Take appropriate corrective actions to address the issues that arise, including amending, replacing, or removing the guideline.

It looks like a lot of work because it is. The realities of supporting the business will more than likely force you to eliminate or severely amend the testing process. "Pay now or pay later" is true for every process involved in quality management. Guidelines that don't work will cause people to lose confidence in the standard, which is a surefire way to render it unusable.

However, there are ways that you could amend the processes and possibly avoid future problems, including:

- Implement guidelines using a phased approach, so you only roll out what's been tested.
- Pilot the standard first and use that opportunity to test the guidelines. It's always a good idea to run a pilot test, especially if you are implementing untested guidelines.
- Only test guidelines that can't be verified through external research. For example, you can make assumptions about some guidelines that have withstood the test of time. Others may need verification through different means.

Finalizing the Standard

In addition to being evidence based and verified, guidelines must be recognized as the legitimate source of truth for the L&D function. Gaining consensus should be a consideration from the project's launch. Therefore, take a collaborative approach that encourages input. There is no one way to build consensus, but facilitate open and transparent discussions among stakeholders, exchange ideas, and encourage active participation. Here are some ideas for building consensus on a standard and its supporting guidelines:

- **Stakeholder engagement workshops.** Facilitate workshops or meetings where stakeholders can discuss the guidelines and the overall standard. Encourage them to participate on a platform that allows open dialogue so they can express their viewpoints, concerns, and suggestions.

- **Working groups and task forces.** Form smaller working groups or task forces composed of representatives from different stakeholder groups who regularly meet to focus on specific aspects of the standard and work collaboratively to address technical details, reconcile conflicting viewpoints, and propose solutions.

- **Consensus surveys and feedback forms.** Distribute surveys or feedback forms to stakeholders to gather their opinions on specific issues related to the standard. They can use the form to rate or rank different options or proposals. Results may reveal areas of agreement or divergence, guiding further discussions and decision making.

- **Pilot projects and demonstrations.** Conduct pilot programs or demonstrations to test the practicality and effectiveness of the standard using real-world scenarios. Stakeholders can then observe the impact of the proposed standard and provide feedback based on their firsthand experiences. Pilot projects can facilitate learning, address concerns, and refine the standard based on empirical evidence and stakeholder input.

- **Create an ongoing collaborative space.** Use an online platform or forum to facilitate ongoing discussions, document sharing, and collective decision making. During the development of the guidelines, online platforms provide a space where stakeholders can engage in discussions and review and comment on draft versions of the standard. I highly recommend having an online home that everyone involved can access for communications and documentation storage.

People invest more interest in a quality management system once they understand how it will influence their lives. Unfortunately, that information may not come until later in the system development process. While the team may be excited to start, interest might wane until the project reaches a point where more specifics can be shared. When this disconnect happens, the team might have to make decisions in the stakeholder's absence or without their full attention that they might later question or outright oppose. This is why ongoing collaboration is necessary and you need to repeatedly build consensus throughout development.

Revising the Standard

Plan time to revise the standard before it's created. Create and communicate a revision process that follows a systematic approach to review, update, and improve the standard over time. There are two types of revisions:

- **Targeted revision** addresses specific items that need to be changed.
- **Scheduled review** can result in possible revisions. For example, you can set a yearly date to review the standard to determine if any changes should be made.

Here are eight steps for creating a revision process:

1. **Define the goals and objectives of the revision process.** Identify the reasons for revising the standard, such as stakeholder feedback, emerging trends, organizational restructuring, or process or procedure changes. Also, set the criteria for changes to avoid confusion with constant updates.
2. **Set a revision schedule.** Determine how often the standard will be reviewed. During the first year or two, reviews should happen more often (possibly twice a year). After that, you may choose to review the standard every few years, but this will depend on a variety of factors.
3. **Establish a revision committee.** Form a committee or working group to oversee the revision process. It could include people who initially helped develop the standard, but getting input from others may also be useful.
4. **Conduct a gap analysis.** For a scheduled review, evaluate the existing standard by comparing it to current industry practices, technological advancements, and user feedback. Identify any gaps or areas that require improvement or updates.
5. **Seek stakeholder input.** Engage stakeholders who are affected by the standard, such as users, industry experts, and internal teams. Collect their feedback, suggestions, and insights on the strengths and weaknesses of the current standard.

6. **Research best practices.** Stay informed about current research, industry standards, and best practices related to the standard's subject matter. Incorporate this knowledge to ensure that the revised standard aligns with the latest advancements and accepted practices.

7. **Use an iterative revision process.** Iterate and refine the revised standard based on the received feedback. Continue to seek input from stakeholders and SMEs to ensure the standard effectively addresses their needs and concerns. Maintain a clear documentation process for all revisions made to the standard. Keep track of changes, versions, and the rationale behind specific modifications. Ensure the documentation is easily accessible and properly organized.

8. **Gain approval and implement the revised standard.** Once it has been thoroughly reviewed, finalized, and approved by the appropriate authorities, communicate it to all relevant stakeholders. Provide guidance on the implementation of the revised standard and any necessary training or resources. Regularly assess its effectiveness and relevance after its implementation. Monitor user feedback, evaluate its impact on processes and outcomes, and make further refinements as needed.

Key Questions to Consider

Before we move on to chapter 7, and you begin developing strategies for supporting your standard and its guidelines, there are a few key questions to consider.

How Far Are You From the Standard Right Now?

When writing each guideline, you should have considered the distance between the guideline and where your team currently is. This understanding will help you determine how much support your team needs to close the gap. That support is the foundation of the quality control policies.

What Current Processes Have to Change?

Leadership does the organization a disservice when they attempt to reassure your team (or gain cooperation) by making promises that there will be no changes in how the team functions. While the changes may not be radical, they will happen and affect people differently depending on their roles. However, you may have to challenge your assumptions about what your team can achieve. As you build your policies, balance optimism with realism about how much change your organization is willing and able to withstand.

How Does the Management of the Team Have to Change?

The L&D leader's role will be most affected as the quality management system is developed and continues to evolve. Quality management requires leadership and oversight. For every guideline that makes it into the quality assurance process and every policy that supports that guideline, leadership will need a strategy to support their team as they try to comply. This is why it's essential to have a process lead. The manager leading the L&D function is still the process owner, but the lead can take on some of the load. Remember, the process lead should be viewed as a collection of tasks and responsibilities, rather than an official role, so you can divide the tasks among multiple people if needed. However, even with a process lead, management must change responsibilities and perspectives to accommodate this new workflow.

How Does the Team's Relationship With the Business Have to Change?

Implementing a quality management system may require changing how the L&D function supports the business. Part of this change is how the team's leadership engages with the organization. Depending on how the function now operates, stakeholders and SMEs may play a big role in the current quality level of your learning experiences. Many enhance the quality by providing useful insights that help you better cater the design to their audiences. But some diminish the quality of the experiences by imposing their own opinions, which may contradict your expertise, and the existing power dynamic provides no leverage for the learning designer to push back.

People outside L&D who negatively affect the course design process may have good intentions, but they're either operating under the assumption that learning and development either doesn't have a body of research and knowledge or not putting much stock in it. Having a documented L&D standard and guidelines can go a long way in winning over business leaders. However, this is only true if L&D leadership finds a way to operationalize the information and consistently communicate it to stakeholders. And they must defend the integrity of the standard and proactively and reactively push back on design and development suggestions that do not comply with it.

How Does the Workflow Have to Change?

Workflow among L&D teams varies, but regardless of how the team is organized, workflow will be affected. People must be prepared for this shift, which we'll tackle in chapter 9.

CHAPTER 7
Controlling Quality

IN THIS CHAPTER:
- Supporting the standard with processes and procedures
- Supporting people as they navigate the quality management system
- Creating quality control tools

Like many of you reading this book, I thought quality control (QC) meant reviewing course materials for errors. I mentioned in chapter 2 that through my research on quality management, I was introduced to the idea that you cannot control the quality of a product once it's finished; you can only control the quality of a product while it's in production. Guidelines assure quality, but you can only follow guidelines if policies, processes, and procedures—which make up your QC measures—are in place to support you during production.

One instructional designer I interviewed said that if you create a QC checklist to follow during the review process, isn't that comparing the course against guidelines? She questioned why all the other steps were necessary if she could make a list and check it at the end. Using a checklist to review a course to determine if it meets criteria is certainly an option for ensuring that products are error free, but it's not a quality management system or QC. It's a checklist. In a quality management system, designers and developers work with the established guidelines and follow supporting policies, processes, and procedures. Even if you supply them with the checklist before they begin working, many will still treat it as a tool to check their completed work.

So, this chapter will not provide you with the ubiquitous QC checklist. Instead, it focuses on supporting quality assurance (QA), or the guidelines that describe quality. This is an important step in building your system—just as the guidelines operationalize the mission, QC operationalizes the guidelines. For example, suppose a guideline says all videos must have closed-captioning. That's great! But is the developer allocated time in the project plan to create the captions? Do they have access to the tools required to streamline the process? And most of all, do they know how to add closed-captioning to an entire course? The answer to those questions is QC.

It's important to note that the guidelines may be enough for some teams to reach their quality standard. Take the closed-captioning example. If your team already knows how to do this, and perhaps has been doing it all along, there may be no need to create processes for it.

Here are some scenarios when I think QC should be limited:

- Your team has a shared understanding of the guidelines and an additional layer of support processes, policies, and procedures is unnecessary.
- Your team agrees to following mandatory guidelines, but each designer and developer interprets them differently. For example, at McCarthan Enterprises, each business line has its own templates for training materials, so the guideline may require designers and developers to use a specific template but allow them to decide what the rest of the screen looks like.
- Leadership believes there is no time to enforce quality at the policy or procedure level. When reviewing a course, the use of a required template will be immediately apparent. However, if there are policies that dictate other details, checking for compliance may take too much time, and some reviewers may not be equipped to take on that task.
- Your team agrees to use processes, policies, and procedures for some guidelines but not others. You may decide that a guideline for closed-captioning needs no further support but the guideline about using templates does because developers have a history of modifying required features (such as colors and logo placement).

Of course, there are consequences for omitting specific QC measures from your system, including:

- You lose the benefit of simplifying onboarding for consultants and new hires. The current team may grow, and having a robust quality management system will streamline how you communicate the team's guidelines and what compliance looks like.
- Too many interpretations of a guideline can potentially make it useless.

- QC protects your system and the people and products within it. As I emphasized earlier, a guideline is just a suggestion if people have no support while trying to follow it.

This chapter focuses on building QC measures to support your guidelines, so let's begin with an explanation of the support model.

The Support Model

I was introduced to support models in the early 2000s when my training team implemented a cloud-based LMS, which was a relatively new thing for the company. The IT department was unhappy about receiving support calls about a system they weren't familiar with that wasn't housed on their servers. They wanted to know how the training team planned to support the new system. After much politicking, we were told to develop a support model. We decided that should be an email address help desk agents could use to forward emails or other messages to a designated person on my team. Since then, I've had to implement support models several times for software and processes.

A *support model* is a framework that outlines how the people engaged in a system will be supported as they comply with the standard. QC is the support model for the standard and its guidelines. For quality management, a support model typically consists of three main components:

- **Support policies** are the support model's foundation, and they are typically the first to be developed among the three. The support policies component of the model outlines the processes and procedures to be followed by everyone involved in complying with the standard's guidelines. A well-defined support policy ensures that issues are addressed promptly and efficiently, facilitating everyone's ability to meet expectations.
- **Support resources** are tools used to navigate the system. They include knowledge bases, frequently asked questions (FAQs), tutorials, and troubleshooting guides. By providing the team with resources that they can access independently, leadership can empower them to investigate and resolve any issues they encounter instead of leaning on process owners and leads for support. Think of resources as support for your policies.
- **Support channels** are the communication channels used to access process resources and other forms of support. By creating multiple

channels, process leaders and owners can provide team members with multiple options for getting the help they need in a timely manner. Think of channels as support for your resources.

Support Policies

First, let's define some key terms. *Policies* are high-level statements defining the team's approach to complying with one or more guidelines. They outline the goals, objectives, and acceptable behaviors related to a specific workflow. Policies are designed to provide a decision-making framework and ensure consistency across the team. They are typically broad, flexible, open to interpretation, and adaptable to different situations.

For example, you may have a preparation policy that says everyone engaging in the system must be prepared to do what they're expected to do. It may include specific details for enforcing the policy, such as providing inexperienced reviewers guidance on how to complete a review. However, the policy should not specify how people are prepared, who will lead the preparation, or when preparation should be completed—only that it must occur.

Policies are supported by *processes*, which are a series of interrelated activities or steps designed to achieve a specific outcome or produce a particular result. They represent the flow of work or tasks required to accomplish a goal and often involve multiple stakeholders, departments, or functions. Processes define the overall sequence, dependencies, and inputs and outputs of activities. They ensure efficiency, effectiveness, and consistency in operations.

To support the example preparation policy, instead of just sending new reviewers course materials and asking for feedback, you can establish a reviewer training process that all reviewers must complete so they better understand their role in the review process.

Processes are supported by *procedures*, which are detailed step-by-step instructions that prescribe the specific actions to take in different situations. They provide guidelines for executing tasks or activities and ensure consistency and efficiency in operations. Procedures are often more detailed than processes, and they offer clear instructions that leave little room for interpretation.

For instance, to support the example reviewer preparation policy, you can use a procedure with detailed information to provide reviewers, including actual training materials with instructions for facilitating the experience or links to online resources.

The person tasked with the day-to-day management of the quality management system is the process lead. Teams can call this role whatever they want—or not give it a name at all. I use process lead in this context because that person will primarily engage at the process level to support the team as processes are carried out per the guidelines. They are not in charge of the policy and are not necessarily required to manage at the procedural level.

The entire quality management system consists of several layers of support. Essentially, no matter what you create, something should support it. In Figure 7-1, the support structure begins with the mission, and everything that comes after it is intended to support that goal. This graphic shows how each component of the system—the mission, standard, guidelines, policies, processes, and procedures—supports the one that comes before it, which is why mission is at the top; everything beneath it supports it. That's also why the arrow is pointing down—you start at the top with the mission. The width of each level also indicates the breadth of each level and, consequently, how much work it will take to create.

Figure 7-1. The Quality Management System Support Structure

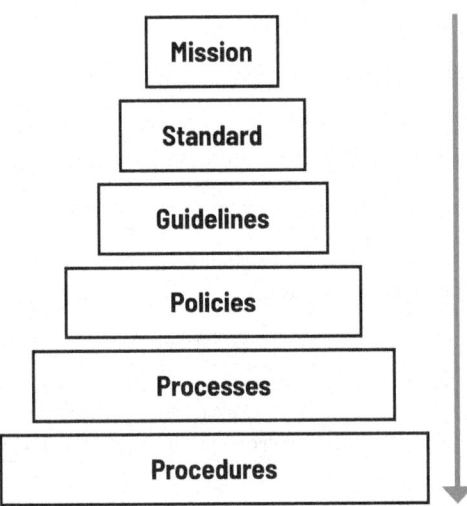

Writing Policies

A policy typically consists of several vital components that clearly and concisely express its purpose, scope, and objectives. While the specific parts may vary depending on the approach and the policy type, there are some common elements, including:

- **Policy title** identifies the subject or area of the policy.
- **Policy statement** is the core component, which articulates the team's stance, principles, or rules regarding the issue. This part is usually clear and concise, outlining the organization's position in unambiguous terms.
- **Purpose statement** outlines the rationale or primary goal of the policy. It explains why the policy exists and what it should achieve.
- **Scope** defines the boundaries and applicability of the policy. It specifies the individuals, departments, processes, or locations covered by the policy. Think through all the possibilities and decide which are important enough to include in the policy.
- **Objectives** outline the specific outcomes or goals the policy should achieve. They provide clarity on the desired results.
- **Exceptions**, if applicable, detail any exceptions to the policy, including criteria for when they can be made.

Table 7-1 outlines one of McCarthan's policies with the different components labeled.

Table 7-1. Example Policy

Policy Title	Sourcing and Selecting Multimedia Components for E-Learning Courses
Policy Statement	All multimedia components used in e-learning courses must come from approved sources, comply with copyright laws, reflect the organization's marketing and branding guidelines, and be accessible to all learners.
Purpose Statement	This policy establishes the criteria for adding multimedia components to e-learning courses, sourcing and selecting them, and recommendations for how they should appear.
Scope	This policy applies to custom e-learning courses designed and developed by the internal L&D team unless otherwise noted.
Objective	The goal of the policy is to ensure e-learning courses developed by the L&D team are consistent and comply with organizational standards.

Table 7-1. (cont.)

Exceptions	Exceptions to this policy may be granted under specific circumstances when the standard guidelines for multimedia integration are impractical or counterproductive to the learning objectives of the course. In such cases, a detailed rationale must be provided and approved by the head of the L&D department. Any exceptions should still strive to meet the overarching goals of consistency, compliance, branding alignment, and accessibility.

Writing Processes

McCarthan Enterprises' policy for sourcing and selecting multimedia components for e-learning courses covers four tasks: getting files from approved sources, complying with copyright laws, reflecting the organization's marketing and branding guidelines, and ensuring accessibility. In some cases, the policy alone may be enough to support the guidelines. The organization's marketing and branding guidelines may be well documented and communicated, and if people know where to find them and how apply them, no further support is needed for that task. However, for other tasks, designers, developers, and stakeholders may need further instruction or clarity. The first task, getting files from approved sources, requires the team to know what "approved sources" means, as well as how to access them and search for and download the desired media. So, more support may be needed for that policy.

As I mentioned, the process supports the policy. The policy shouldn't mention specifics because it provides a high-level structure, whereas the process you need to follow to comply with the policy is more specific. For example, the process for accessing approved sources may be to locate a page on a secured intranet site to locate links and login information. A documented process typically consists of the following components:

- **Process title** provides a concise and descriptive name for the process.
- **Process statement** describes the actions or tasks to be completed, including what needs to be done, who is responsible, and any specific requirements or considerations.
- **Objective** states the purpose or goal of the process. It explains what the process should achieve.
- **Scope** defines the boundaries of the process and specifies the activities, departments, or individuals involved. It clarifies what falls within the scope

of the process and what doesn't. It's possible for different processes of the same policy to have different scopes, but if the policy and process scope are the same, repeating that information is probably unnecessary.

- **Process resources** are any tools, systems, documents, or materials required to carry out the process effectively. This may include software, templates, databases, or other resources necessary for executing the process steps.
- **Roles and responsibilities** are the specific individuals involved in the process and their respective responsibilities. It clarifies who is accountable for each step or task.

Table 7-2 outlines one of McCarthan's processes with the different components labeled.

Table 7-2. Example Process

Process Title	Accessing Approved Multimedia Sources
Process Statement	To access approved multimedia sources, visit the L&D Resources SharePoint page. The sites are listed in alphabetical order along with a description of each site's purpose. Contact the learning technologies team for support.
Objective	This central repository enables every L&D team member to easily identify and access approved sources to ensure that any multimedia included in e-learning courses complies with copyright laws and is high quality.
Scope	The multimedia content can be used for internal learning products for both digital and paper products.
Roles and Responsibilities	Learning designers are responsible for following the process and should use discretion when downloading new files because of licensing limitations. The learning technologies team can provide access to the shared image folder and the most recent job aid. They can also provide additional support if needed.

NOTE

You'll have to decide how to group and categorize processes. Use constraint because too many processes will overwhelm the system development team as well as the system users after implementation.

Writing Procedures

McCarthan Enterprises' process for accessing approved multimedia sources probably provides enough information to support the policy. However, when the team onboards employees and consultants, they may have questions about where the L&D Resources SharePoint page is located. Also, the L&D team does not have full control over the page's location, so the URL might change. Remember, the procedure supports the process, so a documented procedure typically consists of specific steps, instructions, and details for carrying out a particular process. It should include the following components:

- **Procedure title** provides a clear and concise name for the documented procedure.
- **Procedure steps** detail the specific sequence of actions to be performed. Each step provides clear instructions, including any necessary details, tools, or resources required to carry out the procedure.

Table 7-3 outlines one of McCarthan's procedures with the different components labeled.

Table 7-3. Example Procedure

Procedure Title	Accessing Approved Multimedia Sources
Procedure Steps	Follow these steps to locate the approved multimedia sources on the L&D Resources SharePoint page: 1. Open your browser. Your homepage should be the McCarthan Central intranet site. If it's not, navigate there now. 2. On the left-hand side of the homepage menu, click SharePoint. 3. In the Departments section, click HR, and then Learning and Development. 4. Click L&D Resources. If you are not able to access the page, contact the learning technologies team. 5. On the L&D Resources page, select Multimedia from the menu at the top of the page. 6. Review the names and descriptions of the listed sources. 7. Click a source's name to access a link to the site and login information.

How Much Detail Do You Need?

At this point, you may wonder whether all this information is practical to collect and use later. Can't we just go from guidelines to procedures? Is it necessary to add extra layers of information that might overwhelm people and be difficult to track and update? Is it realistic to expect people to comply with guidelines given the nature of the learning design function?

These questions (and many more) are good ones to ask. However, the answers are more likely to be found among your team than from a book whose author is unaware of your circumstances. Remember, there is no sustainable cookie-cutter approach, but the guidance I offer can help you ask the right questions so you can create a system that balances reality with aspirations. Consider that all the information you add is intended to support (or clarify, explain, or expand on) the information that came before it.

Ultimately, you can design the system in any manner that works for your team. The desire to embark on this journey to quality is typically derailed by the amount of work and time involved. However, while anything in this book can be adjusted to meet your needs, development and the transition that follows is never as smooth as it could be. And there are consequences for every choice. Some will be felt immediately while others may manifest later; whether you pay now or then is up to you.

Remember, any system you create will function best when it's supported. So, it's useful to look at everything you're building as a series of blocks that are supported by the ones beneath them. It's also a way to visualize the potential consequences of your choices. For example, your team may only create a mission if you believe that's enough (and maybe it took long enough to gain consensus on that), but people work best if they clearly understand what they can do to fulfill that mission. You can provide that information with a standard and supporting guidelines.

As I mentioned earlier in this chapter, you're free to stop at the guidelines if your team believes that they provide enough information for people to meet the standard. But your guidelines will have less support as people are left to figure out how they'll meet the guideline requirements. And this, of course, affects the mission.

In summary, your system's overall sustainability could be at risk. As Figure 7-2 shows, the less support your system has, the more vulnerable it is to challenges throughout its life cycle. Conversely, the more support your system has, the more stable it is.

Figure 7-2. The Stability Risk of a Quality Management System

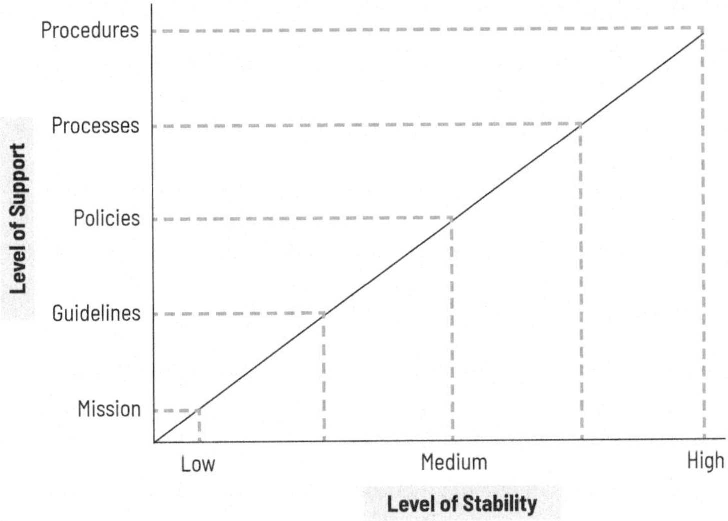

In addition to more support, there are other benefits to adding more layers, including:

- **Making precise modifications.** For example, you can change a process or procedure while leaving the guideline it supports intact.
- **Identifying breakdowns in the system.** If the system is divided into more distinct layers, it's easier to troubleshoot and identify where the problems are.
- **Easily dismantling specific supports.** In some cases, removing support may be easier than building it as you're using it, so consider removing the guideline rather than changing the overall standard.

NOTE

While it's true your system will be more stable if it has more support, it will also be more challenging to maintain. Most support comes in the form of documentation that must be created, categorized, and updated (and those updates must also be communicated). This is why it's important have a rationale for adding each component. You'll have to balance the need for the support resource with the work it will take to maintain it.

Support Resources

Policies are supported by *resources*, or documentation and tools that help people follow the policies. The types of resources that typically need to be created for a quality management system fall into three categories: documentation, job aids, and tools and templates.

Documentation

The quality management system needs to be documented. I suggest you follow document design principles regarding readability and usability. The design of the document will and should evolve. Always test your formatting, which you can do by asking people to complete tasks using the document. For example, ask them to find a specific policy or procedure and time them, or ask them to explain their strategy for finding the information aloud.

Here are a few considerations for documenting your quality management system:

- **Standardization.** Establish a format, structure, and language for documenting quality management policies, processes, and procedures. Standardization ensures consistency and makes it easier for users to navigate and understand the documentation.
- **Process maps.** Use a flowchart or swim-lane diagram to visually represent the sequence of steps, inputs, outputs, and interactions within quality management processes. Mapping provides a clear overview of the entire process and helps you identify bottlenecks or areas for improvement.
- **Document control.** Establish a system to manage versions, revisions, and document distribution to ensure everyone can access the latest versions and minimize the risk of using outdated or incorrect information.
- **Cross-referencing.** Create cross-references and hyperlinks within the documentation to relevant policies, procedures, work instructions, or supporting documents to facilitate navigation and help users find related information quickly.
- **Document reviews.** Implement a review process to ensure accuracy, relevance, and compliance with a standard. The process should include a schedule, the criteria for making a change, and procedures for updating the materials and communicating the changes to the team. To support

continuous improvement, encourage feedback and suggestions from users of the documented processes.

- **Accessibility.** Make the documentation easily accessible to all relevant stakeholders. Consider using an electronic document management system or online platform to enable convenient access and search functionality.

I usually recommend having a single source of truth that contains all the information about the system. The system is a living entity, so its documentation should be stored where it can be accessed and updated as needed. Otherwise, you might run into version control issues. I've seen system documentation stored on online repositories (like Google Drive and SharePoint) that allow you to create and upload documents and other resources.

NOTE

A version control strategy is required for quality management system development and the system itself. There are several strategies for managing versions, like implementing file naming conventions and centralizing where physical and digital materials are stored.

Job Aids

Job aids are another popular resource to help people navigate the quality management system. A *job aid* is a tool or resource designed to help individuals perform specific tasks or activities effectively and efficiently. They should deliver quick reference information, step-by-step instructions, guidelines, or visual aids.

Here are a few considerations for creating a job aid for your quality management system:

- **Understand user needs.** Identify the target audience and their knowledge level, experience, and potential challenges in complying with the process. Conduct user research or engage with SMEs to gain insights into users' requirements and pain points.
- **Keep it simple.** Ensure the job aid is easy to understand. Use plain language, avoid technical jargon, and break down complex information into smaller, manageable steps. Focus on the key actions and critical points that users need to know to comply with the process effectively.

- **Visualize information.** Use visual elements—such as diagrams, flowcharts, or infographics—to present information in an appealing and easily understandable format. Visual aids can help users grasp the process flow, sequence, and relationships between steps more intuitively.
- **Use clear instructions.** Provide concise and action-oriented instructions. Use a step-by-step approach that outlines how to comply with the process. Use a consistent format (such as bullet points or numbered lists) to enhance readability and make it easy to follow the instructions.
- **Highlight critical information.** Identify and emphasize information that users must know to comply with the guidelines. Use document design techniques—such as bolding, highlighting, or formatting choices (like borders, alignment, and proximity)—to draw attention to important points, warnings, or potential pitfalls.
- **Include examples or case studies.** Supplement the job aid with practical examples that illustrate how to effectively comply with the process. Examples and scenarios can enhance understanding and provide context to users, which makes it easier for them to correctly apply the process.
- **Provide references and resources.** Include references to relevant policies, procedures, guidelines, or supporting documents that users can consult for additional information or clarification. Provide links or citations to these resources within the job aid for easy access.
- **Ensure accessibility.** Design the job aid to be easily accessible to users. Consider what format and delivery method best aligns with their work environment. It could be a printed document, a digital file, or an online tool readily available on the company's intranet or knowledge management system.
- **Test and iterate.** Before finalizing the job aid, conduct user testing or gather feedback from a sample group of users. Observe how they interact with the job aid and adjust the document based on their input. Continuously iterate and refine the design to improve its usability and effectiveness.

Job aids are helpful when implementing any change that people are expected to follow independently without close guidance. This is especially true for behaviors that are only needed intermittently. I've often categorized job aids by the development and design process phases and then by topic within the document. For example, a job aid may include guidelines for creating storyboards, as well as sections like planning, writing, and formatting. Each section will also document any corresponding policies, processes, or procedures.

NOTE

You should create job aids based on people's needs rather than what your team thinks they need. This will ensure that you only create helpful job aids. Also, remember that handing your team a thick pile of papers will convey that the system is probably excessively complicated.

Tools and Templates

You can create tools and templates for the quality management system as well as the products you will create with the system. In fact, many templates you may already use are strategies for controlling quality.

Quality management system tools and templates are designed to aid instructional designers and developers in complying with guidelines. When they use tools similar to the items listed here, they are engaged in QC:

- Project intake templates
- Project management tools and templates
- Design and development checklists
- Meeting management templates
- Job descriptions for each role in the quality management system
- SME and stakeholder communication email templates

Product tools and templates are also methods for controlling quality, although they are outputs of the system, not part of the system itself. They include design documents, storyboards, course templates, and presentation templates.

Support Channels

In many cases, L&D templates and tools exist but are difficult to locate or access. Identifying support channels to store and deliver these resources is essential to the system's sustainability.

Limit how many support resources and channels you make available to users. Consider Hicks Law, which states that the time it takes for a person to decide increases with the number of available choices or options. Essentially, the more choices you have, the longer it takes to decide.

There are a few considerations for identifying and creating support channels for your quality management system, including:

- **Research.** Conduct user research to understand the target audience's needs and preferences. Gather insights about their communication preferences, technological literacy, online storage access, and the current channels they use to gather information and seek support.
- **Multichannel approach.** Consider implementing a multichannel approach to cater to different user preferences and needs. Offer a combination of support channels, such as access to the process lead and champions, quality management email inbox, self-service resources and documentation, and online internal communities. This allows users to choose the channel that best suits their needs.
- **Communicate channel types, purposes, and availability.** Clearly communicate the available support channels to users. Provide this information prominently in various ways, like in meetings or other online or in-person community forums. Make it easy for users to find and access the support channels they need.
- **Timely and responsive support.** Ensure that the support channels are accessible and provide timely and responsive assistance to users.
- **Self-service resources.** Develop comprehensive and easily accessible self-service resources to empower users to independently comply with the guidelines. This can include well-organized process documentation, FAQs, video tutorials, knowledge bases, or interactive e-learning modules. Make these resources searchable and user friendly.
- **Feedback mechanisms.** Establish feedback mechanisms to gather user input and gauge satisfaction with the quality management system. Regularly collect feedback through surveys, interviews, or feedback

forms. This helps you identify areas for improvement and make any necessary adjustments to the quality management system.

I have found that how you organize content in the channel is more important than the technology you choose to employ. For example, it doesn't matter how sophisticated your tool is if you don't select and communicate a strategy for when and where to store specific materials. If people can't find them when needed, they'll stop trying to find them. So, develop a folder structure and naming convention, for example, that makes it easy for people to know where to look.

CHAPTER 8
Reviewing for Compliance

IN THIS CHAPTER:
- Exploring the role of quality reviews in the quality management system
- Developing a quality review process
- Designing quality review tools

I've created many quality review (QR) checklists throughout my decades-long L&D career, but none were sustainable. Something was always missing, and I'd find excuses to avoid using it. The checklists typically consisted of common errors I overlooked or design quirks I wanted to avoid. Eventually, I memorized the list and no longer needed it. But the mistakes would soon reappear; I'd create another checklist with a different design, and the cycle would begin again. Once I realized that I was missing a process for the checklist to support, I found it easier to discard the tool.

When I started researching and writing about quality management, I thought the result would be the perfect review checklist. I realize now that we focus too much on checklists and the review process. Although reviewing for accuracy is essential, some of the effort needed to create and manage processes to review against guidelines can instead be put into enhancing the design and development phases with more QC support so that you're more likely to meet guidelines during production. The quality review then becomes just one tool of many that you can use to support compliance. Honestly, simply having guidelines, policies, processes, and procedures will go a long way.

Your team may decide to work within the system you've created for a while before adding a robust review process. This strategy can help everyone understand which guidelines need the additional support a review process provides. There are other strategies as well, and you can be creative with integrating quality reviews into your system if you choose to do so.

In this chapter, we'll explore the QR process and how you can make it work for your team.

What Is a Quality Review?

A *quality review* (or *inspection*) is the systematic process of evaluating a product, service, or work output to determine compliance with predefined standards or guidelines. It involves carefully comparing an item against established guidelines or specifications. A review can be conducted at different stages of production, meaning you can review the design document, storyboard, and developed course materials. However, most energy is usually devoted to the later stages of course development. The review may involve a visual examination, course walk-throughs, testing, or specialized tools or equipment to ensure accurate evaluation. Reviewers may follow checklists, test plans, or specific testing protocols to ensure consistent and objective assessments.

The findings of a quality review help identify any quality issues so corrective actions can be taken to improve the product. Reviews also help ensure that the final output meets the required quality guidelines and upholds the mission. Quality reviews play a role in promoting learner satisfaction, maintaining consistency, and continuously improving the quality of the learning experiences your team creates.

Review vs. Test

Review and *test* are often used interchangeably when I ask practitioners for details about their existing quality management processes. Often, reviewers simply take or complete the course as a learner would, which is neither a review nor a test. Reviewing, testing, and completing a course are distinct tasks that result in different outcomes.

As I mentioned earlier, a *quality review* is a process of evaluating a product or service based on predetermined criteria. It involves assessing various product or service aspects to determine if it meets the desired quality levels described in the guidelines. Reviewers are typically asked to examine the product against established quality criteria for functionality, visual design, accessibility, accuracy, usability, and compliance. Of course, they're also asked to identify errors, defects, and other areas for improvement.

The outcome of a quality review is typically a completed tracker, checklist, or report that includes findings, recommendations, and corrections that designers and developers can use to update the course. The review process identifies potential issues during the development life cycle, allowing for timely corrective actions.

A *quality test*, on the other hand, refers to verifying and validating a product's quality through testing activities. It involves executing various processes to ensure the product or service functions as intended, meets the specified requirements, and performs as expected.

Testers are typically given *test plans* (a road map for the testing process), *test cases* (a specific set of conditions, inputs, and expected results intended to verify the functionality and quality of a system), or *test scripts* (instructions that list the steps the reviewer should follow to execute a specific test case). Testers use various techniques and methodologies depending on the nature of the product. Quality testing aims to detect defects, errors, or any issues affecting the product's functionality, reliability, or overall quality. Testers execute test cases, record the results, and compare them against expected outcomes. They report results to those who can address the issues and make necessary improvements. While reviewers compare the course to guidelines, testers focus more on documented expectations.

Here's one way to think about it: Reviewing a course focuses on what you see, while testing focuses on what you may not see. Let's consider feedback for multiple-choice questions, for example. Designers and developers need to know if the question, the options, and all the answer feedback meet guidelines and are accurate. They also need to know whether the mechanics of the question function as anticipated. Reviewers can provide most of what's needed, like assessing the accuracy of the question and the answers. But they might need to be instructed to reload a slide repeatedly and answer questions multiple times so they can see what feedback appears for all answers. Some reviewers will do this intuitively, but most will do only what they're asked. They often instinctively take the path of least resistance, and testing inherently deviates from the path most traveled to nooks and corners of the course that were overlooked by the person who built it. Testers must reload multiple-choice questions and play out scenarios to determine if the feedback is correct and the question works as anticipated.

Reviewers and testers have a role in your quality management system. The stakeholders and team members checking courses throughout development are obligated to be thorough, but they will likely be too busy to complete a comprehensive testing process. A review shouldn't be viewed as an incomplete test because reviews are also valuable. The point is to be clear on what you need, who can provide it, and how you can prepare them to do so. A reviewer can provide a high-level view of course accuracy and user experience compared against the guidelines, while a tester can provide a comprehensive assessment of whether the course functions as anticipated.

Whether you need reviewers, testers, or both is your choice. Of course, with strapped resources, it may not feel like a choice. As with all the roles in the quality management system, it's essential to focus more on the role's responsibilities rather than what it's called. You are free to allocate responsibilities to different people on the team. For example:

- Reviews can be conducted by people outside the L&D team (such as stakeholders and SMEs), while testing remains in-house.
- Develop criteria for prioritizing which courses receive comprehensive testing (such as visibility or complexity).
- Create tools and templates to automate the review and testing processes to make them easier and less time consuming.

Regardless of how you implement reviewing and testing, both functions must be designed and documented. Use that documentation to prepare people to take on these roles with confidence.

NOTE

This book focuses on the review process, although testing strategies are provided throughout this chapter.

When Should a Quality Review Occur?

Reviews inform the design process. They are not report cards intended to check how well a designer did their job. Reviews help the design team make informed decisions about how a learning experience can meet stakeholder expectations and comply with the standard. So, the review process needs to happen while there is still an opportunity to make adjustments.

Some reviews happen throughout the design and development process, and typically assess accuracy and functionality. However, a *quality review* focuses on guideline compliance. It is often more comprehensive, well documented, and time consuming, so conducting one too early in the process is not advised because errors may distract from it. The most common time to conduct documented quality reviews is immediately before the pilot program (or a trial or test run of a new program before it is fully implemented or offered to a broader audience). This is an opportunity to gather feedback, assess the effectiveness of the course content and structure, and identify any necessary improvements or adjustments before officially launching the course.

Scheduling quality reviews around pilot programs is common because that's the point at which courses are nearing completion but unfinished enough to still be changed. The learning designers and developers also engage in the quality management system as they use the guidelines throughout the design process, so a quality management system is about more than just reviews.

The QR Process

Developing a review process can be as complex and nuanced as the process itself. Before you begin, here are three things to keep in mind: the goal of the QR process, timing, and preparing reviewers.

The Goal of the QR Process

The primary reason for the QR process is to communicate to designers and developers how the course can better comply with the guidelines. A *compliance indicator* refers to how reviewers share their assessment, whether it's through narratives, rubrics, or ratings. (I'll discuss compliance indicators in more detail later in this chapter.)

I've had clients who wanted to include space for reviewers to offer positive feedback on how well the course meets the guidelines. They feared that no one would want all bad news. I agree. However, one of the benefits of creating guidelines is that it makes feedback less personal because it focuses on guidelines (which designers and developers should be supported in achieving) instead of the designer's abilities. For example, when I take on a project with no guidelines, I make decisions based on my education and experience. So, when I received negative feedback early in my career, it felt like my education and experience were being questioned. If there are guidelines in place, I know what's expected of me and what to do if I don't meet them. In addition, adding more information to the review process will slow it down.

If you are receiving feedback that your review process is focusing too much on what's wrong with courses, I recommend adding space in the review documentation for overall impressions or high-level pros and cons.

Timing

The first thing many people want to know when they are invited to a party is how long they'll have to stay! Wondering how much time it will take to complete a review is natural, but not a question that's easily answered. Obviously, the more thorough your process, the more time it will take to complete. Therefore, the QR process will need to balance the review's goals with the typical reviewer's limited time.

One strategy is to have multiple review levels with varying scopes. Perhaps they are called *basic review* and *comprehensive review*—something to distinguish them from one another. However, you'll need to develop criteria for when materials are eligible for each review level.

I also recommend developing time estimates based on class characteristics. For example, you can start with a baseline estimate for reviewing (and documenting) a 45-minute e-learning course (approximately 60 minutes) and then add increments (15 to 30 minutes) based on course characteristics, like the amount of interaction and multimedia elements.

Preparing Reviewers

You can create temporary reviewers but not temporary editors, instructional designers, and multimedia developers. In other words, if you have to teach what a guideline means and its purpose to the reviewer before they can provide feedback, you need a different reviewer or you need to remove the guideline from the QR process. Designers and developers don't often get to choose who reviews the courses they create, let alone assess each reviewer's ability to do so. As a result, you should have a strategy in place for preparing reviewers.

We often assume people know what is expected of them when we ask them to review materials. In my experience, reviewers prefer more information than less, but if you overwhelm them with too many instructions, they probably won't read them. They don't want to spend time guessing what you want, especially if you plan to change the overall approach to reviewing courses. Remember, asking people to compare course elements to guidelines differs from just fielding their opinions.

Use the same strategies to prepare reviewers as you would for any other role. You should:

- **Set expectations for the review experience.** Communicate the goals, objectives, inputs, and outputs of the QR process. Be clear on the estimated time commitment.
- **Clearly define the reviewer's role and importance.** Provide a comprehensive overview of the reviewer's role on the team and in the organization. Explain how their work contributes to the overall success of the project and the company. Emphasize their value to the team by ensuring product quality, satisfaction, and reputation. Keep in mind that it's possible to just have SMEs and other non-L&D stakeholders focus on accuracy reviews. They can still give their opinions on the course's quality, but they won't be asked to compare the course to any guidelines. The guideline reviews may exist as an internal function only.
- **Provide a supportive environment.** Reviewers are so valuable to the course development process that we should ensure they have a pleasant experience and celebrate their role in the project. Strive to create a positive and supportive culture in which reviewers are comfortable expressing their opinions, concerns, and ideas. Encourage open communication channels and active listening from the L&D team.

- **Provide training and resources.** As I previously mentioned, people want helpful information communicated in an easy-to-use format. Offer resources (such as documentation, guidelines, and best practices) to equip quality reviewers with the necessary skills and knowledge to efficiently navigate the process. Demonstrating your investment in the reviewer experience will make them feel valued and prepared for their responsibilities. We'll tackle a quality reviewer guide later on in the chapter.

Transforming Guidelines Into Review Criteria

At this point, you have guidelines and policies to support those guidelines. But how do you turn them into review criteria for the QR process? In some ways, it's as easy as turning a statement (the guideline) into a question. For example, if the guideline says to add closed-captioning to all courses with a voice-over, then the review item could be, "Is all the voice-over content close-captioned?"

In other cases, the transformation process may be more complicated. Returning to the McCarthan Enterprises case study, let's use two guidelines developed by Asia's team as examples for turning guidelines into review criteria. You can follow a similar process with your team.

McCarthan's Learning Objectives Guideline

Guideline LD 2.0 says, "Write learning objectives that target a single behavior using the ABCD (audience, behavior, condition, degree) format, omitting elements when they're assumed or not applicable." For the guideline to be met, the following information must be present:

- **A learning objective.** The learning objective must be visible to the reviewer.
- **Each learning objective targets a single behavior.** The reviewer must be able to recognize whether the objective is targeting one or multiple behaviors.
- **The ABCD components.** The reviewer must look at a statement and identify all four components. One of the ABCD components can be omitted under certain conditions, so if one is missing, the reviewer must make a judgment call on whether its absence is justified.

Given these factors, fellow learning designers are best equipped to accurately compare this objective to the guideline, which leaves you with four options:

1. Change the guideline to include what can be reviewed by any reviewer.
2. Keep the guideline intact but scale it back in the reviewer guide.
3. Create multiple review guides, one for reviewers who are learning designers and another scaled-down version anyone can follow.
4. Omit the guideline from the review process. (Remember, there's always the option to omit a guideline from the quality management system entirely.)

Asia's team chose the second option because they believe having a guide for the learning designers to use as they design may be effective enough in most situations. So, their review criteria will check for the following:

- **The objectives are present in the course.** Asia and her learning design lead debated the need for this criterion. The learning design lead believes that the learning objectives are for the designer and can be replaced with more simplified goals in learner-facing materials. Asia likes that idea, but she wants the team to keep the objectives in the course because it's the only time she or the learning design lead can view them since they are not heavily involved in every designer's projects. They can revisit the idea once they both have confidence that everyone can consistently write objectives.
- **Each objective targets a single behavior.** They agree to define what this means for reviewers outside learning and development.

Sometimes, using a scaled-down version of the guideline is sufficient for review criteria so that a wider variety of reviewers use it to determine compliance. Note, however, that the designer is still required to be fully compliant as instructed by the original guideline.

McCarthan's Readable Fonts Guideline

Guideline VD 1.0 says, "Ensure text is readable by using legible, nondecorative fonts. Use a font that remains legible in different sizes and on different devices. For presentations, ensure the text is large enough to be read from the back of a large room."

To determine whether the course meets the guideline, the reviewer must be prepared compare what they are seeing against the guideline. For example:

- **Nondecorative fonts.** The reviewer must be able to distinguish decorative and nondecorative fonts.
- **Text remains legible in different sizes and on different devices.** The reviewer must view the course on multiple devices to prove this.
- **For presentations, text can be read from the back of a large room.** The reviewer has to view the presentation from across the room to prove this.

Any reviewer could objectively compare the course's characteristics to the guideline in this case. The challenge is that part of the guideline requires viewing the course on alternate devices, which likely won't happen. This leaves you with four options:

1. Change the guideline to include what can be reviewed by any reviewer.
2. Keep the guideline intact but scale it back in the reviewer guide.
3. Create multiple review guides, one for reviewers who are learning designers or on the learning technology team and another scaled-down version for anyone can follow.
4. Omit the guideline from the review process.

Asia's team chose option three. While their original plan was to have only one review type, they realized they would need different versions for some guidelines. They still want everything reviewed, but understand that people outside of L&D may struggle.

So, their review criteria will check for the following:

- **Nondecorative fonts are used throughout the course.** The learning design lead must include the following definition: A nondecorative font is plain (without any unique visual flair or decorative elements) and clearly readable. Arial and Times New Roman are nondecorative fonts.
- **The font size is legible.** This criterion now only applies to the device the reviewer is using.

They decided to support compatibility with other devices through policies and procedures. This means they will include a policy that supports this guideline (learning designers must check for the legibility of their chosen font on other devices), if applicable. The procedure will then provide instructions on doing it themselves or partnering with the learning technology team.

Ultimately, reviewer constraints (logistical, technical, or otherwise) may require you to use multiple versions of review criteria. The samples in this section provide insight into transforming guidelines into review criteria. I find that it's helpful to look at each guideline or policy and view and use it from a reviewer's perspective. Consider whether the typical reviewer can objectively and accurately assess compliance based on the type of learning experience that will be sent through the review process. You may also test your quality review tools with reviewers before and during piloting the system to solicit their feedback on what to change to make the process easier.

Quality Review Tools

Once you have established your criteria based on your guidelines and policies, you can organize them using a QR tool. Reviewers use the tool to communicate their assessment through *compliance indicators*, which are narratives, metrics, or measures used to determine adherence to the guidelines. It can serve as a quantifiable marker that indicates whether specific requirements or criteria have been met.

There are three considerations when selecting an approach to assessing compliance:

1. The review process must produce actionable feedback.
2. The indicators must be simple enough for reviewers to use.
3. The approach should stay consistent throughout the review tool. In other words, avoid using different compliance indicators in each section.

There are four common approaches to compliance indicators: rubrics, checklists, rating scales, and narrative descriptions. Let's explore the pros and cons of each one.

Rubric

A rubric is a scoring guide that outlines specific criteria and performance levels for each. Design guidelines can be converted into a rubric, which reviewers can use to assess how close the course is to complying with standards.

Pros:

- Provide clear criteria and performance levels, which offer a structured framework for assessment.
- Promote objectivity and consistency by providing a standardized method of evaluation.

Cons:

- Quantifying complex aspects of course quality in this way may oversimplify the review process and fail to capture nuances.
- The rubric's structured nature may limit flexibility when assessing course designs that don't fit neatly into predefined categories or criteria.

Checklist Assessment

A checklist is a simple tool that lists the design guidelines as individual items. Reviewers can use a checklist approach to assign binary values (such as yes or no) or numerical values (such as zero or one) to indicate the presence or absence of specific design elements outlined in the guidelines.

Pros:

- Offer a straightforward and easy-to-use option.
- Promote standardization by providing a predefined set of criteria.

Cons:

- Different reviewers may prioritize different elements, which can lead to variability in the assessment process and potentially overlook important quality indicators.
- Ease of use may cause reviewers to move through the list too quickly.

Rating Scales

Reviewers can use rating scales to assign numerical scores to different aspects of the course design. They can be based on specific criteria outlined in the design guidelines. For example, reviewers can rate the course on a scale of one to five for elements such as instructional clarity, engagement level, multimedia integration, or assessment effectiveness. The cumulative scores provide a quantitative measure of how well the course aligns with the guidelines.

Pros:

- Provide a quantitative measure by assigning numerical scores or ratings to different aspects or criteria.
- Promote flexibility because rating levels or scales can be customized based on the specific criteria and design elements.

Cons:

- Rating scales may lack the precision required to differentiate between closely ranked scores.

- Reviewers may experience *anchoring bias*, which occurs when initial ratings or anchor points influence subsequent ratings.

Narrative Description

The narrative description approach requires reviewers to provide descriptive feedback to assess how much a learning experience aligns with the guideline instead of relying solely on numerical scores or checklists.

Pros:
- Allow for contextualized explanations, which may offer a holistic understanding of how closely the course adheres to guidelines.
- Facilitate communication between reviewers and course developers because detailed feedback helps learning designers understand the rationale behind it.

Cons:
- It can be time consuming for reviewers to write the narrative descriptions, as well as for the learning designers to interpret them.
- Absent a standardized structure, it may be challenging for learning designers to understand what is being asked of them.

When selecting a compliance indicator, remember that it must communicate to the designer what needs to be changed. Balance the need for that information with the time it will take for reviewers to record their feedback.

At McCarthan Enterprises, Asia's team initially decided to use a Likert scale because its rating scale would indicate how close a course was to compliance. After talking with the learning designers and potential reviewers and doing further research, however, they realized that the Likert scale would not yield clear, actionable data.

Instead, the team decided to take the following approach:

1. Create a quality reviewer issue tracker in SharePoint.
2. Use a checklist with a partial Likert scale for guideline-specific feedback. (They liked the checklist's simplicity but also wanted to include the Likert scale's choices. So, each item will need to be assessed by checking yes, no, partial, or other.)
3. Provide space for narrative description feedback for partial or undetermined answers.

Most of my clients use Microsoft Excel as a quality review tool, but I do not condone this strategy. Excel is not a word processor and shouldn't be used as such. I encourage you to invest in tools that allow you to create issue trackers (such as SharePoint) so you can easily enter and format text, yet still filter and sort the feedback. If you are reviewing e-learning courses, you can also use the review tools that come bundled with your development software.

Writing Criteria

When you write the criteria, use the style of your chosen compliance indicator. Table 8-1 provides an example issue tracker that Asia's team uses.

Table 8-1. Sample Issue Tracker

Criteria	Yes	No	Partial	Other	Feedback	Recommendation
Learning Design						
The objectives are present in the course.						
Each objective targets a single behavior.						
Visual Design						
Nondecorative fonts are used throughout the course. *A nondecorative font is plain (without any unique visual flair or decorative elements) and clearly readable. Arial and Times New Roman are nondecorative fonts.*						
The font size is legible.						

McCarthan's Quality Review Process

When and how your team conducts a QR process depends on how your team is organized, your team's design process, and the resources available to you. This section uses McCarthan's example to explore what should happen before and after the process.

Before Review

The project manager (PM) creates the project plan and, with the project's learning designer (LD), facilitates a kick-off meeting with the project team. During the meeting, the PM and LD explain the project details and deliver the quality reviewer training presentation. After the meeting, the PM sends the team links to the quality reviewer materials folder on SharePoint, the quality review issue tracker, the quality reviewer guide, and the reviewer welcome letter.

Once the LD completes the version intended for quality review submission, they upload the files to SharePoint and send the link to the PM. Depending on the course, the PM may conduct an initial review of the course materials and work with the LD to make updates and upload new versions. The PM emails the project team using the review kick-off email template, which includes a link to the course materials, quality reviewer materials, and the quality reviewer issue tracker.

After Review

After the review trackers are submitted, the PM and the lead SME review the feedback and compile an actionable list of changes for the LD. If anyone involved has questions or concerns, the PM schedules a meeting to discuss the actionable list. Otherwise, depending on the project and the team's needs, the LD either updates the course materials and uploads them to SharePoint or incorporates the changes and moves on to the next stage of development.

Review Process Materials

Several materials are needed to complete the QR process, such as the quality reviewer training presentation, welcome letter, issue tracker, guide, and kickoff email template. Most of them are intended to prepare reviewers to engage in the review process. Let's explore each one in greater detail.

Quality Reviewer Training Presentation

Before the QR process begins, you'll want to explain it using a *quality reviewer training presentation*, which is a resource designed to teach individuals or teams about the process, reviewing principles, and how to assess the quality of products, services, or processes within an organization. It aims to provide guidance on how to effectively evaluate and provide feedback to ensure adherence to quality standards and drive continuous improvement. It's an essential part of onboarding training for reviewers.

At McCarthan Enterprises, the onboarding training program is about 45 to 60 minutes long. You can use the example outline in Table 8-2 to create a session for your team.

Table 8-2. Sample Quality Reviewer Training Outline

Training Topic	Time
1. Introduction • 1.1. Brief overview of the importance of QR and its impact on organizational success • 1.2. Session agenda outline	5 minutes
2. Understanding QR • 2.1. QR definition and purpose • 2.2. Importance of QR in maintaining standards and driving continuous improvement • 2.3. The role and responsibilities of a quality reviewer	5 minutes
3. QR Framework • 3.1. Introduction to QR the framework and criteria • 3.2. Explanation of how the framework aligns with organizational standards, customer expectations, and regulatory requirements • 3.3. Overview of key elements and components of the QR framework	15 minutes
4. Review Process and Methodology • 4.1. Step-by-step explanation of the QR process • 4.2. Introduction to tools and checklists that can be used during reviews	15 minutes
5. Providing Constructive Feedback • 5.1. Importance of constructive and actionable feedback for improvement • 5.2. Tips and best practices for providing feedback in a clear, specific, and actionable manner	10 minutes
6. Q&A and Wrap-Up • 6.1. Open the session for questions and answers • 6.2. Summary of key takeaways and closing remarks	10 minutes

Guidance for Reviewers

A key component of quality reviewer training is providing guidance on conducting reviews. You must be clear on what you want reviewers to do. Some reviewers will simply read the materials or complete the online course, so they will only encounter the problems they encounter. Others will go out of their way to complete random and unnecessary combinations of tasks, which could be helpful or unhelpful, depending on what you're looking for.

<blockquote>

NOTE

Make sure that reviewers understand what the terms included in their reviewer materials mean. For example, you may need to describe what terms like "engagement" and "actionable" mean and what they look like in the context of a course. Again, you can exclude specific course characteristics from the review process for certain or all reviewers if you believe they are unprepared to make a proper assessment.

</blockquote>

What you tell reviewers depends on your desired outcome. The guidance listed here includes suggested strategies that reviewers may find helpful. Advise them to do the following.

Before:
- Begin by thoroughly familiarizing yourself with the preset guidelines. Ensure you understand the criteria and how they apply to the training materials.
- Participate in the prereview meeting to clarify any questions about the guidelines, materials, or review objectives.

During:
- Read through the training materials once without making judgments to get an overall understanding of the content and structure.
- Then, perform a detailed review, exploring the materials more closely against each guideline. If necessary, take notes and document your observations before adding your comments to the review tool.
- Use the provided standardized tool or template. Follow the instructions, and ask for help or clarity when needed.
- Keep the target audience in mind. Consider whether the materials are suitable for their knowledge and experience level.
- Evaluate engagement and interaction. Look for elements in the materials that promote active learning and participation.

- Consider whether the materials are accessible to all learners, including those with disabilities, and the content is inclusive and culturally sensitive.
- Provide actionable recommendations. Your feedback should be constructive and offer specific suggestions for improvement.

After:

- Participate in follow-up meetings to discuss findings with other reviewers, resolve conflicts, and finalize the review.

Quality Reviewer Welcome Letter

Before the QR process begins, the PM should email a quality reviewer welcome letter—which is a formal communication for individuals who have been selected or assigned to be quality reviewers for a specific project or process—to the reviewers selected by the project team. It serves as an introduction and provides important information to the reviewers regarding their role, responsibilities, and expectations. The letter aims to create a positive and welcoming environment for the reviewers and to establish clear communication channels. Here's an example you can use.

Subject: Welcome to the Team

Dear [reviewer's name],

We are thrilled to welcome you as a quality reviewer for [project, process, or organization name] at [your organization]. Your expertise and commitment to maintaining high-quality standards make you an invaluable addition to our team.

During your tenure as a quality reviewer, you will be involved in reviewing [relevant documentation or process name] and assessing compliance with established quality standards. As a quality reviewer, your input is vital in identifying areas for improvement, providing valuable feedback, and supporting our goal of continuous improvement. Your keen eye for detail and analytical skills will greatly contribute to maintaining and enhancing the quality of our [project, process, or organization name].

To assist you in your role, we will provide any necessary resources and support throughout the review process. Our team is readily available to address any questions or concerns you may have. Please feel free to reach out to [contact person's name] at [email address and phone number].

We value your dedication and expertise, and we are excited to have you as an integral part of our quality review efforts.

Thank you for your commitment and contribution as a quality reviewer. We look forward to a productive collaboration.

Sincerely,

[Your name]
[Your title and organization]

Quality Review Issue Tracker

Before the QR process begins, the LD should send a link to a *quality review issue tracker*, which is the tool reviews will use to communicate their feedback to designers and developers. You can create one using cloud-based software or other desktop applications; you just need to ensure that it's accessible and editable for reviewers. The tracker serves as a centralized platform for capturing, documenting, and monitoring issues that require attention or resolution. (Table 8-1 shows an example issue tracker.)

Asia's team at McCarthan Enterprises used SharePoint for their tracker. They built it to include the information and datapoints—which should be represented as columns—that will inform the design process. Asia's team records the following datapoints, which you should consider adding to your tracker:

- **Issue ID.** A unique identifier or number assigned to each issue for easy reference and tracking.
- **Module.** The specific course or module that the issue pertains to (this will help you organize issues by course components).
- **Screen or page.** The location where the issue can be found or that the issue pertains to (this will help you organize issues by course components).
- **Criteria.** The criteria that the learning experience has meet.
- **Yes.** A checkbox for indicating that the course meets the criteria.
- **No.** A checkbox for indicating that the course does not meet the criteria.
- **Partial.** A checkbox for indicating that the course partially meets the criteria.
- **Other.** A checkbox for indicating that the designer and developer should look for more details in the feedback column.
- **Feedback.** Space for narrative feedback from the reviewer (you can set your tracker up to require feedback from reviewers in this box if they select the no, partial, or other checkboxes).
- **Recommendations or actions.** A column to document the recommended actions or solutions to address the identified issues (this will help you track the steps taken for issue resolution).

- **Priority.** A classification or rating that indicates the seriousness or impact of the issue on the course's quality or learning outcomes (this will help you prioritize and allocate resources accordingly).

Quality Reviewer Guide

Before the QR process begins, the PM should send the reviewers a link to the quality reviewer guide, which is a comprehensive document or handbook for reviewers to reference to ensure consistency and effectiveness when conducting quality reviews and assessments. A typical quality reviewer guide includes, but is not limited to, detailed instructions for the review process and job aids for best practices.

Detailed Instructions for the Review Process

The instructions will differ based on the system you've built but will typically include:
- Instructions for accessing and using the quality review issue tracker.
- Details for each criterion, if necessary. The criteria statement in each line item in the tracker may provide enough information for the reviewer to make an assessment.
- Instructions for their part in the review process from start to finish. (This should include details about everything from accessing the tracker to submitting information to meeting with the team to discuss the feedback.)

Job Aids for Best Practices

The guide may also include job aids for how to successfully engage in the review process. Talk with your team and potential reviewers to gain insight into where reviewers may need help. For example, knowing how and when to deliver feedback can be challenging. Adding a feedback best practices job aid may help. It should include the following suggestions for reviewers:
- **Be specific and objective.** Reference examples, instances, or sections within the course materials. Avoid general or vague statements that may be difficult for the designer to understand and address.

- **Focus on improvement.** Frame feedback in a constructive manner, emphasizing areas for improvement rather than just pointing out flaws or errors. Offer suggestions or alternative approaches to help address identified issues and enhance the overall quality of the course. However, confer with your colleagues to ensure your suggestions are accurate.
- **Maintain a professional tone.** Use a respectful tone in your feedback. Focus on the course materials rather than personal opinions or judgments. Remember that the goal is to help improve the course, not to criticize the course designer or instructor.
- **Provide clear explanations.** Explain the rationale behind your feedback if it's not obvious. This helps the course designer or instructor understand the reasoning and make informed decisions about potential revisions.
- **Offer actionable recommendations.** Instead of simply identifying issues, offer specific suggestions or solutions.
- **Follow the review process guidelines.** Adhere to any guidelines or protocols for the course review process. This includes using the designated channels or platforms for providing feedback, meeting established deadlines, and following any specific formatting or submission requirements.
- **Be responsive and open to discussion.** Remain open to further discussion regarding your feedback. Encourage the course designer or instructor to seek clarification and provide additional context if needed. Engage in a constructive dialogue to ensure a thorough understanding of the feedback and facilitate effective revisions.

Quality Review Kickoff Email Template

Before the process begins, the PM should email the project team using the review kickoff email template, which is a communication tool that provides essential details, guidelines, and expectations. You can use this message to formally announce and initiate the QR process. Creating a prewritten email template can save you time and ensure consistency across different projects.

Here's an example you can use:

Subject: Quality Review Kickoff: Join Us in Enhancing [*Project, Process, or Organization Name*]

Dear [*review team or reviewers*],

We are excited to officially kick off the QR process for [*project, process, or organization name*]. Your involvement as a quality reviewer is pivotal in our collective effort to ensure high-quality outcomes and drive continuous improvement.

    I want to personally thank you for your dedication and commitment to the review timeline. Your timely feedback will enable us to address any challenges and ensure smooth progress toward our goals. Our team can support you if you require any assistance or resources.

    I extend my heartfelt appreciation for your contribution as a quality reviewer on behalf of the entire [*project, process, or organization name*] team. Your efforts will significantly influence our success, and I am confident that, together, we will achieve remarkable outcomes.

Sincerely,

[*Your name*]
[*Your title and organization*]

CHAPTER 9
Questions From the Field

IN THIS CHAPTER:
- Common concerns about developing a quality management system
- Strategies for getting commitment and support from your team and the organization
- Customizing the system to accommodate a variety of limitations

While reading through the recommendations in this book, you may have questioned how they will work in your organization—or anyone's organization. It's a fair question because the L&D function can take on different forms, and what quality management looks like can vary.

You should be skeptical, but make sure that skepticism is pointed in the right direction. If your team is creating products—and L&D materials are products—you will benefit from even the most rudimentary quality management system. There's no avoiding it. As I mentioned several times in earlier chapters, your team already uses some informal system to maintain quality, even if it's entirely reactive or retroactive.

So, the skepticism should be focused on the timing of development and implementation, the system's complexity, and whether the team is ready and willing to take on the challenge. But make no mistake—creating a robust quality management system is a long-term investment in your organization, products, and people. Whether you believe that investment is worthwhile is up to you.

In this chapter, I'd like to tackle some of the most common questions I get when discussing quality management with L&D professionals. Then, at the end, I'll wrap up the story we began in chapter 3 with Asia and the McCarthan team.

First Things First

Most questions center around whether assembling a quality management system is worth it. To some, it feels like a disproportionate response to preventable typos. For others, this is a project they've wanted to take on for ages. Here's how I typically answer the questions I receive about getting started.

How Can I Be Sure This Will Be a Worthwhile Project to Invest In?

If your team produces products in any form, you need a way to ensure the quality of those products. The question is how robust and efficient the system must be to make it worthwhile and whether you have the time and resources make it happen.

You must assess your organization's current state and determine whether the benefits of building a system are worth it. For example, if after an investigation, the team concludes that the only problem is typos instead of poor learning design, perhaps it's not worth it. However, typos may be the manifestation of a deeper issue that needs to be addressed. And, maybe the courses could use a redesign to better meet learners' needs, but people are reluctant to express their concerns after the project reaches a certain point in development.

Conducting research and understanding how everyone handles quality provides helpful information for quality management and any other process improvement or upskilling endeavors.

When Will We Begin to See the Benefits of the System?

Seeing early wins is essential to the success of any project. During the planning phase, identify the incremental wins and think about how to achieve and communicate them. You may realize some benefits before the system is in place. Some examples of potential early wins the organization might experience include:

- Understanding the L&D function's strengths and weaknesses
- Documenting new and existing processes so they are easier to review, update, and improve
- Improving communication with stakeholders and SMEs around expectations before, during, and after the course development process
- Gaining insight into opportunities for upskilling practitioners as they collaborate on guidelines to support the standard
- Increasing L&D team collaboration and knowledge sharing through discussions about individual processes

How Can We Develop a Quality Management System With Limited Resources?

If you don't have enough resources to develop a system that supports the team and your organization, then quality is probably being compromised somewhere. Consequently, you may need a system more than an organization with more resources.

Always consider *how* you can make this work instead of *if* you can. Once you shift your thinking, you may unlock creative possibilities for implementing the system. As I mentioned in the introduction, the goal of this book is not to simply implement the system, but to use its guidance to investigate your current state, develop goals, and work toward those goals using the resources available within the limitations specific to your organization.

Focus on the tasks rather than the roles and titles. Remember, you can divvy up and share responsibilities in a variety of ways.

I Am a Team of One. How Can I Do This Alone?

You can develop a quality management system that works for you. It's just a series of supports. Recall Figure 7-1, which explained the quality management system's support structure. You can stop at any level, depending on the amount of support your system needs.

I often work alone on my company's products. Before I knew how to build a stable system, I would begin at the process level. However, I wouldn't follow the processes for long because they were only based on how I felt at the time. When my needs (or mood) changed, I made new processes. When looking for older files, I often unearthed *template graveyards*—old templates that never saw the light of day because I had moved on by the time I finished them. I eventually learned that all my random processes had failed because they weren't tied to a larger system to support them.

After learning more about quality management, I realized all I needed was a mission and a standard with guidelines. I only needed to go down to the policy and process level for guidelines when I hired other people for support so they'd know my expectations. Prioritizing my system components this way saves me from writing processes and procedures I don't need. I use the guidelines to streamline my design decisions and communicate my design approach to SMEs and stakeholders.

Why Go Through So Many Steps?

If you think you would get the same list of reviewer criteria from just making a list off the top of your head, it's true. You will probably end up with the same checklist, but that's not a quality management system. The process described in this book aims to help you develop a comprehensive system that the checklist is only a small part of. Chapter 7 provides more insight into the differences between a quality review checklist and a quality management system.

Can We Do This If No One on My Team Is Trained in L&D?

Yes, and your team is a perfect candidate for this process. An excellent way to enter any profession is to learn what's expected before developing bad habits. However, while I suggest you avoid using a standard to teach learning design, you can use it to identify which skills your team needs. For example, as you develop the guidelines, you must consider whether your team is proficient enough to comply. If not, you may need to proactively get them the support they need.

Developing the System

The next set of questions focuses on developing the system. These stem from justifying the amount of work and clarifying the recommended steps and overall system design.

The System Is Too Complex for Us to Design and Maintain. How Can We Make It More Realistic?

I can't stress enough that this journey belongs to your team, and the system resulting from your effort is uniquely yours. There is no one-size-fits-all quality management system. Various factors will influence how robust and complex your system will be, including company and team size, team organization and workflow, and the products you develop. Therefore, create a system you can maintain by considering how you will create, manage, and update each component (such as the process or documentation) before you create it.

This is why I suggest adopting a quality-first mindset. Approach each recommendation by considering how it can work instead of assuming it can't. There are many ways to shrink or grow a system like this by altering factors like scope, processes, or guidelines.

How Long Will This Take to Develop?

It's a good idea to embrace continuous development. The system is alive and will keep evolving. During the planning stage, identify different implementation stages to work toward. You can break it down by:

- **Modality.** Only include e-learning solutions.
- **Product.** Only include print materials, like leader and participant guides.
- **Client.** Only include learning experiences for services departments, like HR and IT, instead of client-facing teams, like sales.
- **Team member.** Only include learning experiences created by specific team members.

Using this approach will provide quick wins and data on handling future quality management system implementations.

What Can We Do to Stay on Track?

Assume disruptions will happen and incorporate them into your development and implementation plan. Be realistic about how much you can accomplish during a specific timeframe. The responsibility for getting things done falls on the process owner and process lead. The team looks to them to determine priorities. But leaders can't claim that the project is a priority and then load the team down with other work without adjusting the timelines to accommodate the project. For example, suppose leadership decides the team will devote one day a week to developing the system. In that case, timelines for incoming projects may need to be adjusted and may take longer than usual.

One strategy is to break the project into phases rather than assuming you'll tackle the entire thing at once. If you look at each phase as a separate project, you'll have less anxiety about losing momentum. You can use the project plan sections as phases like this:

- **Creation.** This step includes creating the system and the four phases: quality planning (creating standards), quality assurance, quality control, and quality review (three months).
- **Pilot program.** Select learning experiences to use as part of a pilot program for the new system. It's essential to have identified and realistic criteria to evaluate the results (six months).

- **Evaluation.** Evaluate the pilot program's success against the established criteria (one month).
- **Revision.** Revise the system based on the evaluation's results (six months).
- **Launch.** Officially launch the first iteration of the quality management system (one month).
- **Integration.** During this period, the process leads will be focused on encouraging people to use the system so it can go from being an interesting experiment to the new normal (one year).
- **Adoption.** The goal is to get to full adoption, meaning the system is stable and only needs periodic scheduled revisions (ongoing).

Or you could use the natural breakdown of the system as phases:

- **Phase 1. Quality Planning.** Create the standard.
- **Phase 2. Quality Assurance.** Create guidelines to support the standard.
- **Phase 3. Quality Control.** Create policies and procedures to support the guidelines.
- **Phase 4. Quality Reviews.** Create a mechanism to check for accuracy and ensure guidelines and their supporting policies and procedures are followed.

I prefer breaking down the system in phases because it's a more natural approach to spreading the work over time.

We Can't Assign a Process Lead. Can We Divide the Responsibilities?

The process lead role is the one people find most challenging to accommodate. But I argue that a process lead is necessary. Once the quality management system is launched, the process lead manages and oversees the system and often engages in improvement initiatives throughout its life cycle. Consequently, they are also responsible for gathering feedback, identifying areas that need improvement, and developing strategies to optimize processes.

In addition, another one of their key responsibilities is supporting the L&D team members and others who serve as SMEs and reviewers. This will require managing system documentation, collecting and sharing tips and tricks, and communicating any updates made to the process.

Many teams may forego assigning the process lead role due to a lack of resources. Some believe that once the system is developed, everyone involved should be responsible for their own journey to compliance and there should be no need for oversight. I argue that every system with multiple components needs oversight. Remember, what gets watched gets done. If no one monitors or watches the process, you risk it fading away.

However, what's important isn't the title—it's the responsibilities. You can scale, modify, and distribute them in a way that works for your team.

We Can't Assign a Process Owner. Can We Divide the Responsibilities?

The process owner is, and will always be, the L&D lead. They are responsible for the system's development, growth, and maintenance. This responsibility cannot be delegated. As I've noted throughout this book (and others have proven in quality management research), senior leadership's support and guidance is required for the system's survival.

After implementation, the process owner is responsible for:

- **Monitoring and controlling.** The process owner works with the process lead to monitor the system to ensure it is effective, efficient, and meets the organization's objectives. They also implement and support controls to mitigate risks and ensure compliance with guidelines. During system revisions and improvements, they will approve (or know about) all major decisions. They will also resolve conflicts and encourage any stakeholder participation requested by the process lead.
- **Managing stakeholder expectations.** The process owner manages stakeholder expectations by ensuring the process lead has a mechanism for informing them of the system's progress and any issues. They also work to keep stakeholders engaged throughout the system's life cycle and assure them that their contributions to the discussion are valuable.
- **Supporting continuous improvement.** The process owner works with the process lead to continuously improve and optimize the new process to ensure its effectiveness and efficiency.
- **Advocating for the system.** The process owner supports quality management by advocating for the continued existence of the system. They should be the system's greatest champion with an unwavering, quality-first mindset.

How Can I Convince My Team We Need This?

Make the case by explaining how the system can support team efficiency and effectiveness. Use storytelling and data to develop a case study that explains how having a system can positively influence the project.

Many teams won't get through the quality management system's development process on the first try. As I mentioned in chapter 5, the project often gets deprioritized. It's also an exercise in change management, so you will encounter resistance along the way that may be too much to overcome. Also, if it seems too big, it's easy to get overwhelmed.

If the project does not have enough support to power through challenges, examine why. If you look closely, you might learn or confirm insight into how your team functions. Again, it is important to stress that your team already has a quality management system, and you may learn that the existing system is robust enough to support your mission. If so, you can avoid creating a solution in search of a problem. In that case, it's still worth discussing the system's ability to scale so it can accommodate organizational changes, survive staffing and procedural adjustments, and be documented in some form.

If you've discovered that you can't move forward due to challenges in the team's organization, communication, morale, or leadership, then there should be little doubt that the team is compromising quality in some way. While the problem may be bigger than what you and your colleagues can tackle, just bringing your research about challenges within the team to leadership's attention may be alarming enough to trigger changes. It should be troubling that a team that helps other teams document and train their processes cannot do the same for themselves. However, there is no time wasted if you turn what you learn about the L&D function at your organization into action.

We Can't Agree on a Mission. What Do I Do?

First, understand that any resistance you encounter is likely a symptom of a more significant problem. If promoting the system's benefits is not enough to get people on board, the underlying problem may be too big to tackle.

I believe that the driver of resistance is often the fear of losing something. Consider how these changes could affect each person's work or even their roles as team members. The change makes them feel vulnerable in some way that you're not addressing.

A lack of trust can also drive resistance. For many organizations, new initiatives that are supposed to change the way they do business constantly come and go. We do so much work to launch a program, and it just fades away, leaving nothing positive in its wake. Why should they trust that this program will last?

Consider how you can handle the quality management system's launch differently than past initiatives. A common concern is a lack of transparency, so be as communicative and inclusive as possible to assuage those fears.

We Agree on a Mission but Disagree on the Details. What Do I Do?

The more specific the information, the more difficult it will become to reach a consensus. The details involve people's daily work lives, which means they'll be more passionate about the specifics. Break up the work to avoid tackling everything at once and use what you've learned as best practices for future implementations. For example, ask for people to volunteer and let the most enthusiastic group create a smaller system to test. More people may get on board once they see their co-workers' commitment and success.

Life With the Quality Management System

This last group of questions pertains to ones I commonly receive from people who are interested in what might come next, once you've developed a quality management system.

Can We Force Our Vendors to Comply With Our Guidelines?

No, you cannot legally force vendors to comply with a quality management system standard unless compliance is explicitly outlined in their contractual agreement. Vendors, like freelancers, are independent contractors, not employees, which means they operate with a significant degree of autonomy and are not subject to the same level of control and oversight.

However, there are some key actions you can take to support vendor compliance, including:

- **Add terms to the contractual agreement.** The vendor contract terms should explicitly state any quality management standards, expectations, or deliverables that the vendor must meet. If both parties agree to these terms and they are included in the contract, the vendor can be legally obligated to comply with them. You can also add them to the scope of work.

- **Add language regarding dispute resolution.** Include provisions for dispute resolution in case there are disagreements regarding the quality of work or compliance with quality standards. Mediation or arbitration clauses can help resolve such disputes. While disputes are unlikely to escalate to the point when legal recourse is needed, consider adding language to the contract that explains what will happen if a vendor continuously fails to meet the quality standards or other contractual obligations. Consult with legal counsel to understand your options in such cases.

My Learning Designers Are Resistant to Standardization. What Can I Do?

After working in learning and development as a learning designer for decades, it's been my experience that most learning designers resist standardization. Learning design is treated more like an art than a science, which is one reason why initial discussions are so important. Ask people what characteristics this system should have to encourage their compliance.

Note that standardization in quality management ensures consistent and uniform quality by establishing documented practices, procedures, and criteria. Products should consistently comply with guidelines, and unless those guidelines dictate overall appearance, object positioning on slides, or content structure, all courses don't need look the same. You can absolutely build a system that's flexible enough to accommodate individual expression, but still intentional about that design and development.

My Team Wants to Pick and Choose When and How They Will Engage With the System. What Can I Do?

It's worth repeating that quality management should not be used as a punitive measure. In other words, you shouldn't use it to identify people who are falling short or to punish them for noncompliance. Deming (1982) says, "85 percent of the reasons for failure are deficiencies in the systems and process rather than the employee. The role of management is to change the process rather than badgering individuals to do better."

So, view the system as the source of resistance to full compliance rather than the employee. In other words, always look to the system first. If it's not the system, it may be the environment in which the system operates. Engaging with the quality management system is only one workflow among many, and perhaps you must make adjustments in other areas. A noncompliant team member may have great ideas for how to make the system easier to sustain. Next, look to leadership. Is leadership reinforcing compliance as a priority?

Finally, there will be people who resist because they want to, but that is also a symptom of a more significant problem that needs to be addressed with an individual outside the scope of the quality management process.

Wrapping Up With Asia and the McCarthan Team

Let's say that Asia and her team at McCarthan Enterprises launched their quality management system one year ago. They decided that the system's scope should include e-learning courses for only one retail business line. Before developing your system, consider some lessons learned from Asia's experience.

Balance Empathy for the Team With the Business's Needs

Asia approached the quality management system as an additional process, but it quickly became the most prominent process in the team's workflow. She managed with a quality-first mindset, and the team's conversations became rife with the system's lingo. While quality was a priority, she didn't want the team to feel like robots or cogs in a big machine. So, she worked to balance empathy for her team with the needs of the business and the quality management system.

Refine a Consistent Message About the Value of Quality Management

The review process needed more support than Asia anticipated. Before implementation, her biggest concern was how to handle noncompliance from the L&D team. Instead, she was surprised to find the most resistance from the reviewers.

After some discussions, the team identified two issues. First, the reviewers didn't know what was expected of them, and messaging was not consistently provided to them. Also, there were no consequences for noncompliance.

In response, the learning design lead, Jabari, created an online module to teach reviewers about their role in process. He did so to ensure consistent messaging and to have the ability to track who completed the reviewer training course. Asia also used the tracking data to discuss the issue with her vice president. She worked with them to determine how this information could encourage accountability.

The team had to refine their messaging regarding the value of the review process to the organization. Asia also recognized that not initially doing so was a setback in the L&D team's efforts to gain more respect in the organization.

Have a Rationale for Each Layer of Support the Team Creates

The team created all the guidelines, policies, and procedures needed to support quality management for the e-learning courses in the retail business line. The team valued the policies, but the procedures were too difficult to maintain because people handled them in different ways and the technology they used often changed. The team discussed abandoning procedures and ending the support chain at policies. Asia realized the team should focus on providing a rationale for each layer of support they created rather than building them all early on just because they thought they should.

Conclusion

A quality management system is essential to the L&D function. It's designed to ensure that the learning experiences the team produces support the organization as intended. However, implementing a quality management system is not a one-time task. It is a continuous process that requires ongoing attention and dedication. Quality management involves constantly evaluating and improving your team's guidelines and the policies, processes, and procedures that support them to ensure they can work as efficiently and effectively as possible.

Creating a quality management system is not merely about compliance and metrics; it's about fostering a quality-first mindset that values growth, embraces inclusion, and promotes a culture of continuous improvement. A quality management system is not a rigid framework set in stone, but a dynamic process that evolves with our workforce's changing needs and aspirations. It is an ongoing journey of refinement, driven by our unwavering dedication to creating meaningful and influential learning experiences.

Remember, it's not about if you can create a quality management system—only how.

Acknowledgments

While this book reflects my insights and interpretations from my time working in L&D, it's also a tapestry woven with the expertise, experiences, and knowledge of many. It is with immense gratitude that I acknowledge the contributions of my colleagues and the invaluable insights provided by each person with whom I discussed quality management. Their experiences and perspectives have been the bedrock of this work, providing depth, nuance, and a multifaceted view of the topic.

I am grateful to the numerous professionals and experts I had the privilege of interviewing for this book. Their willingness to share their experiences, knowledge, and perspectives enriched it immeasurably, offering a comprehensive and nuanced understanding of the subject matter. These conversations were enlightening and pivotal in highlighting the diverse approaches and innovations within the talent development field.

A special acknowledgment goes to the Association for Talent Development (ATD) and The Learning Guild. These organizations have been foundational to my journey in the L&D profession, providing invaluable resources, networks, and opportunities that have significantly influenced my thinking and writing on quality management. Their commitment to advancing the profession and fostering a community of learning professionals has been a constant source of motivation and has undoubtedly enriched the content of this book.

In navigating the complexities of research and writing, the guidance from my professional network has been a beacon of light. Their expertise and generosity in sharing their time and knowledge helped make this book a personal and collective achievement.

Reflecting on bringing this book to fruition, I am reminded that such endeavors are never solitary pursuits. To everyone who has played a part in this journey, your impact extends beyond the pages of this book. Thank you for your contributions, for believing in the value of this work, and for helping bring it to life for readers everywhere.

Appendix

This appendix has three worksheets:

- **Asia's Getting Started Worksheet.** In chapter 3, you were introduced to Asia and her team at McCarthan Enterprises. Use her completed worksheet as an example.
- **Getting Started Worksheet.** Use the blank version as a guide to develop a quality management system for your team.
- **Project Plan Outline.** Chapter 5 discussed building a project plan for creating a quality management system. Use this outline to create one.

Asia's Getting Started Worksheet

1. How many characteristics of a formalized process does your team's approach to quality management meet? Select all that apply.

✓	Characteristic
☐	Governed by a mission or goal
☐	Equipped with guidelines to measure against
☐	Informed by documented policies, processes, procedures, and terms
☐	Designed to be scalable and flexible
✓	Supported by tools and templates

2. Which review model does the team primarily use now?

✓	Model
☐	Internal dedicated team (Dedicated is defined as a team that only works on quality issues for an L&D team)
☐	External dedicated team
☐	Peer review (with other learning designers)
✓	Self-review

3. Briefly describe your existing quality management system.

> For each project, the review team consists of the designer, SMEs, and possibly other stakeholders. For the design document, storyboards, and instructor-led materials, learning designers email them to the review team. We used to ask that feedback be added to an online spreadsheet, but most reviewers never used it and just used track changes, so we stopped asking. The learning designer reconciles the feedback through conversations with SMEs and stakeholders. For e-learning materials, the review team for each project uses online review software. Again, it's up the learning designer to reconcile any conflicts. If there's an issue, they escalate the problem to me. We don't have a set number of reviews. We keep doing it until we get it right. Unfortunately, errors still slip through.

4. What issues are you addressing by implementing a quality management system?

1. The business leaders and learners are complaining about the quality of the courses in retail.
2. The learning experience design team doesn't know what expectations they need to meet.
3. The business leaders want a voice in the training process and want to know what to expect from the training team.

5. What's driving your need to address these issues now?

There's no one driver, but there is pressure on me to at least understand why problems are increasing. I am concerned that if things continue as they are, our team will be more vulnerable to cuts in the future. Outsourcing the training function or cutting it to bare bones and contracting out the rest have been floated as possibilities. When I accepted my role, the vice president of operations said I was the training team's last hope—although now he says he was joking. There's a rumor that the manager I replaced was aggressively encouraged to retire. I don't know what to believe and don't want to make decisions based on fear. The training team wants to service the organization in the best way possible. There's no deadline, but at the same time, it's overdue. I'm also new to learning and development and I hope building this process will help me learn more.

6. Who will be involved in the design of the quality management processes, and what role will they play?

Name	Project Role	R, A, C, I*	Current Role
Asia Douglas	Process owner	A	L&D manager
Jabari Foster	Process lead	A	Learning design lead
Jamie McIntyre	Project manager	R	Project manager
Uma Patel	SME	C	L&D business partner, retail
George Allen	SME	C	Regional manager, Southeast
Alonzo Reid	SME	C	Regional manager, Midwest
Eddie Hernandez	SME	C	Learning technology specialist
Juwan Jackson	SME	C	Learning facilitator, retail
Chris Weinburger	Team member	R	Administrative assistant
Karma Singleton	Team member	R	Training coordinator
Alice Tran	Sponsor	A	Vice president, HR
Daniel Rivers	Sponsor	I	Vice president, retail operations

*R = responsible—people who do the work to complete the task; A = accountable—the person ultimately accountable for the correct and thorough completion of the deliverable or task (can also be understood as the approver or final approving authority); C = consulted—people (such as SMEs) whose opinions are sought, and with whom there is two-way communication; I = informed—those who are kept up to date on progress, often only on completion of the task or deliverable, with one-way communication.

7. When would you like to implement the process?

We need a draft of the system in three months. We will implement it over time.

8. What is driving that date?

Everyone involved wants to see changes sooner rather than later. We have large projects starting soon, and I think they may be good candidates for testing the new system.

9. What resistance might you encounter?

The most resistance will probably come from the learning design team. They will be affected the most. Jabari says the team will resist a standard that forces them to do everything similarly. He previously tried to institute templates, but team members always had an excuse not to use them. I also think the business partners will resist because they believe they are the face of the department and take the most heat for any changes in the process. Ultimately, people will resist change and the unknown.

10. What project and communication tools do you hope to use throughout the process? If the tools are online, can you ensure everyone has access?

To manage the project, we'll probably use SharePoint. Many outside online tools are blocked on our laptops.

11. What barriers do you anticipate encountering?

Besides resistance, time. I don't know how to prioritize this when we have so many competing projects. So, we'll need to keep focused on the benefits. Otherwise, it won't work.

12. What types of materials do you plan to create quality processes for?

Good question. I assumed all of retail; however, as I answer more of these questions, I think maybe we should start small either by including all materials for one retail business or just including the e-learning courses for the entire organization. I'm not sure.

Getting Started Worksheet

1. How many characteristics of a formalized process does your team's approach to quality management meet? Select all that apply.

✓	Characteristic
☐	Governed by a mission or goal
☐	Equipped with guidelines to measure against
☐	Informed by documented policies, processes, procedures, and terms
☐	Designed to be scalable and flexible
☐	Supported by tools and templates

2. Which review model does the team primarily use now?

✓	Model
☐	Internal dedicated team (Dedicated is defined as a team that only works on quality issues for an L&D team)
☐	External dedicated team
☐	Peer review (with other learning designers)
☐	Self-review

3. Briefly describe your existing quality management system.

4. What issues are you addressing by implementing a quality management system?

1.	
2.	
3.	

5. What's driving your need to address these issues now?

6. Who will be involved in the design of the quality management processes, and what role will they play?

Name	Project Role	R, A, C, I*	Current Role

*R = responsible—people who do the work to complete the task; A = accountable—the person ultimately accountable for the correct and thorough completion of the deliverable or task (can also be understood as the approver or final approving authority); C = consulted—people (such as SMEs) whose opinions are sought, and with whom there is two-way communication; I = informed—those who are kept up to date on progress, often only on completion of the task or deliverable, with one-way communication.

7. When would you like to implement the process?

```



```

8. What is driving that date?

```



```

9. What resistance might you encounter?

```



```

10. What project and communication tools do you hope to use throughout the process? If the tools are online, can you ensure everyone has access?

```



```

11. What barriers do you anticipate encountering?

```



```

12. What types of materials do you plan to create quality processes for?

```



```

Project Plan Outline

Goals and Objectives

-
-
-

Project Scope

Project Deliverables

-
-
-

Project Timeline

The timeline from creation to launch may include the following steps:

Step 1. Creation

- Phase 1. Quality Planning. Create the standard.
- Phase 2. Quality Assurance. Create guidelines to support the standard.
- Phase 3. Quality Control. Create policies and procedures to support the guidelines.
- Phase 4. Quality Review. Create a mechanism to check for accuracy and ensure guidelines and their supporting policies and procedures are followed.

Step 2. Pilot Program

List any upcoming learning experiences that can be used as part of a pilot program for the new system. Establish realistic criteria to evaluate the results.

Step 3. Evaluation

Evaluate the pilot program's success against the established criteria.

Step 4. Revision

Revise the system based on the evaluation's results.

Step 5. Launch

Officially launch the first iteration of the quality management system.

Step 6. Integration

Encourage people to use the system so it can become the new normal.

Step 7. Adoption

The system is stable and only needs periodic scheduled revisions.

Resource Plan

List and define key roles and responsibilities:

- [Role]: [Responsibilities]
-
-
-
-

RACI Chart

Task or Activity	Responsible	Accountable	Consulted	Informed

Risks

Risks	Assessment	Mitigation	Risk Monitoring and Control

Budget

Item	Amount	Details
Direct costs	$	
Indirect costs	$	
Contingency funds	$	
Budget allocation	$	
Total budget	$	

Reporting Plan

Communication Plan

Item	Details
Communication goals	
Communication channels	
Communication frequency or schedule	
Communication content	

References

Biech, E., ed. 2022. *ATD's Handbook for Training and Talent Development.* Alexandria, VA: ATD Press.

Deming, W.E. 1982. *Quality Productivity and Competitive Position.* Cambridge, MA: Massachusetts Institute of Technology, Center for Advanced Engineering Study.

Desikan, S., and R. Gopalaswamy. 2006. *Software Testing: Principles and Practices.* Pearson India.

Duffy, G.L., and S.L. Furterer. 2020. *The ASQ Certified Quality Improvement Associate Handbook.* Milwaukee, WI: Quality Press.

Gravells, A. 2016. *Principles and Practices of Quality Assurance: A Guide for Internal and External Quality Assurers in the FE and Skills Sector.* Thousand Oaks, CA: SAGE Publications.

Hoyle, D. 2011. *Quality Management Essentials.* New York: Routledge.

Kotter, J.P. 2012. *Leading Change.* Boston: Harvard Business Review Press.

Oakland, J.S., R.J. Oakland, and M.A. Turner. 2021. *Total Quality Management and Operational Excellence: Text With Cases,* 5th ed. New York: Routledge.

Neelen, M., and P.A. Kirschner. 2020. *Evidence-Informed Learning Design: Creating Training to Improve Performance.* London: Kogan Page.

Pyzdek, T., and P.A. Keller. 2013. *The Handbook of Quality Management: A Complete Guide to Operational Excellence,* 2nd ed. New York: McGraw Hill.

Roberts, H., and B.F. Sergesketter. 1993. *Quality Is Personal: A Foundation for Total Quality Management.* New York: Free Press.

Stamatis, D.H. 2016. *Quality Assurance: Applying Methodologies for Launching New Products, Services, and Customer Satisfaction.* Boca Raton, FL: CRC Press.

Training Industry. 2020. *Lead the Change: CPTM Workbook.* Training Industry.

Vance, D.L., and P. Parskey. 2021. *Measurement Demystified: Creating Your L&D Measurement, Analytics, and Reporting Strategy.* Alexandria, VA: ATD Press.

Walton, M. 1986. *The Deming Management Method: The Bestselling Classic for Quality Management!* New York: TarcherPerigee.

Williams, R. 2008. *The Non-Designer's Design Book*, 3rd ed. Berkeley, CA: Peachpit Press.

Yablonski, J. 2020. *Laws of UX: Using Psychology to Design Better Products and Services*. Sebastopol, CA: O'Reilly Media.

Index

Page numbers followed by *f* and *t* refer to figures and tables, respectively.

About the Author

Hadiya Nuriddin is a highly accomplished and award-winning L&D professional. She's known for her extensive expertise in educating professionals to enhance their job performance. Her qualifications include a master of education in curriculum design and a master of arts in writing and publishing from DePaul University, where she graduated with distinction. She also holds a bachelor of arts in English from Michigan State University.

Her key qualifications are diverse and comprehensive, encompassing learning strategy consultation, instructional and curriculum design, e-learning development, webinar development and delivery, project management, artificial intelligence utilization, learning technologies implementation, and quality management system design.

Since March 2008, Hadiya has been leading Duets Learning as the owner, senior learning strategist, and senior instructional designer. In this role, she specializes in consulting with both small and large organizations to improve performance through various learning solutions, including online, classroom-based, blended, and on-the-job methodologies. Her accomplishments include developing e-learning and instructor-led solutions for clients in a variety of sectors, such as banking, finance, insurance, technology, retail, pharmaceutical, professional services, oil and energy, media, nonprofit, and association management. She's also won two talent development awards: ATD's Talent Development Outstanding Professional Award and The Learning Guild's Guild Master Award.

In addition to her professional endeavors, Hadiya has an impressive background in facilitation. She has taught workshops for ATD Education since 2017, covering topics like writing for instructional design and training and e-learning instructional design. Her academic experience includes designing and leading courses at Southern New Hampshire University, Triton College, and the University of San Diego.

Hadiya also holds several certifications, including the Certified Quality Improvement Associate (CQIA) from the American Society for Quality, Certified Professional in Training Management (CPTM) from Training Industry, Certified Change Practitioner from Prosci, Certified Virtual Facilitator from the International Institute for Facilitation, and Certified Professional in Talent Development (CPTD) from ATD.

Hadiya is also an accomplished author. Her previous book *StoryTraining: Selecting and Shaping Stories That Connect* was published by ATD Press in 2018. She wrote two issues of *TD at Work*: "Get the Whole Picture With a Performance Assessment" and "Power E-Learning With Stories." Hadiya also authored a chapter in *ATD's Handbook for Training and Talent Development*, "Delivering as if Learning Depended on It." In addition, she maintains an active role in the learning community as a presenter at conferences held by ATD, The Learning Guild, and *Training* magazine, and has helped organize the Chicago eLearning & Technology Showcase since 2012.

Hadiya's career is a testament to her dedication to the L&D field, marked by her significant impact on both organizational performance improvement and the broader learning community.

About ATD

The Association for Talent Development (ATD) is the world's largest association dedicated to those who develop talent in organizations. Serving a global community of members, customers, and international business partners in more than 100 countries, ATD champions the importance of learning and training by setting standards for the talent development profession.

Our customers and members work in public and private organizations in every industry sector. Since ATD was founded in 1943, the talent development field has expanded significantly to meet the needs of global businesses and emerging industries. Through the Talent Development Capability Model, education courses, certifications and credentials, memberships, industry-leading events, research, and publications, we help talent development professionals build their personal, professional, and organizational capabilities to meet new business demands with maximum impact and effectiveness.

One of the cornerstones of ATD's intellectual foundation, ATD Press offers insightful and practical information on talent development, training, and professional growth. ATD Press publications are written by industry thought leaders and offer anyone who works with adult learners the best practices, academic theory, and guidance necessary to move the profession forward.

We invite you to join our community. Learn more at **TD.org**.